YOUTH SPORTS GUIDE
For Coaches and Parents

Edited by: Jerry R. Thomas
Louisiana State University
Baton Rouge, Louisiana 70803

Editorial Consultant:
Albert Warson
Toronto, Canada

Published by:
The Manufacturers Life Insurance Company
and The National Association for Sport and Physical Education

*Manu*Life /NASPE

©1977 **The Manufacturers Life Insurance Company**
and **The National Association for Sport and Physical Education**

Second Printing June 1978
Third Printing June 1979
Fourth Printing June 1980
ISBN #0-9690538-1-9
Library of Congress Catalog No. 77-83343

Copies of this book are available from
AAHPERD Publications, 1900 Association Drive
Reston, Virginia 22091
    Stock Number 245-26046
Discount 5% on orders for 10 or more copies.

Contents

Chapter 7
Winning Isn't Everything Nor Is It the Only Thing!
Walter E. Cooper, University of Southern Mississippi

Foreword

This coaching guide is the result of a joint effort by the National Association for Sport and Physical Education and The Manufacturers Life Insurance Company. For the past few years NASPE has explored the role of a professional association in influencing the organized youth sports programs in North America. A special NASPE Youth Sports Task Force met in June 1976 to focus on this issue and recommended that the association develop a publication translating current research into information useful to volunteer coaches and easily understood by parents of young athletes. NASPE and ManuLife have answered that need.

ManuLife's collaboration with NASPE is an excellent example of international cooperation in the field of education and personal development. The enjoyment of sports is universal and lifelong. We hope this guide will enrich that experience.

S. Jackson

E.S. Jackson
President
The Manufacturers Life
Insurance Company

R. D. Merrick

R.D. Merrick
Executive Secretary
National Association for Sport
and Physical Education

Preface

This book was planned at a national meeting in Washington, D.C., January 18th and 19th, 1977, when participants (see page 5 for list) developed the outline and reached a consensus about the goals of youth sports:

1. *To provide varied opportunities to develop specific motor skills associated with many sports.* Children should be exposed to a variety of sport opportunities, with increasing emphasis on performance as the child matures.

2. *To provide opportunities to practice wholesome competition.* Competition is part of the American lifestyle. But undue importance should not be attached to the outcome of this competition with young children. Skill development and the opportunity to participate should be stressed. Parents and coaches should encourage the child to judge his/her performance according to ability, rather than the outcome of the contest. As children mature, the outcomes of contests can become more important.

3. *To provide many opportunities for social interaction.* Youth sports offer many opportunities for desirable social development within and among families. The game enables families to get together and interact with others, which leagues and coaches should encourage. Social events, such as picnics and covered dish suppers within both a team and a league, contribute to family togetherness and desirable behavior of all those involved in youth sports.

We would like to emphasize that youth sports programs are for all children. While leagues must be structured according to skill and maturation, youngsters should all be able to participate at some level on a regular basis. In our opinion, a "regular basis" is in *every* game and practice session. In many sports, particularly among pre-teenagers, there is little reason for separating boys and girls. However, these decisions are generally made at the community level. Regardless of whether boys and girls play together or separately, the opportunities to play must be equal. Racial considerations *should not be factors* in opportunities for youth sport participation.

Communities must also increase opportunities for handicapped children to participate in youth sports. Some of these children may not be able to participate with non-handicapped children, but equal opportunities should be provided nonetheless. We endorse the inclusion of handicapped children in regular youth sport leagues where possible.

Several terms used in this book should be defined:

1. *Coaches* — most frequently a volunteer parent, but also including paid coaches and older youth players who coach younger players.

2. *Competitive* — regularly scheduled sports events for children and youth, organized and supervised by adults.

3. *Youth Sports* — competitive games for children and youth, usually 8 to 18 years of age.

This manual presents a rare opportunity for youth sports because it collects and translates research information. This manual does not imply any criticism of current practices by any youth sport group. We assume any group involved in youth sport wants to help children. We share that common objective. We have tried to take the best data available and help you use it to provide a better sport experience for children. Let's make sports fun and enjoyable for everyone, but most especially *good for all kids!*

Jerry R. Thomas
Editor

Members of the Planning Committee

Lucy Burkett
Shaker Heights City School District
Shaker Heights, OH 44120

Ronald Byrd
University of Alabama
Birmingham, AL 35294

Walter E. Cooper
University of Southern Mississippi
Hattiesburg, MS 39401

Warren Giese
University of South Carolina
Columbia, SC 29208

Charles Hall
American Junior Bowling Congress, Inc.
Greendale, WI 53129

Margie Hanson
American Alliance for Health,
Physical Education and Recreation
Elementary Education
Washington, DC 20036

Joe Henson
3468 Mildred Drive
Falls Church, VA 22042

Gordon Jeppson
National Association for Sport
and Physical Education
Washington, DC 20036

Luke LaPorta
Liverpool Central School
Liverpool, NY 13088

Ranier Martens
University of Illinois
Urbana, IL 61801

Ross Merrick
National Association for Sport
and Physical Education
Washington, DC 20036

G. Lawrence Rarick
University of California
Berkeley, CA 94720

Marie Riley
University of North Carolina
Greensboro, NC 27412

William Savage
Fairfax County Public Schools
Falls Church, VA 22044

Vern Seefeldt
Michigan State University
East Lansing, MI 48824

Robert Singer
Florida State University
Tallahassee, FL 32306

Jerry Thomas
Louisiana State University
Baton Rouge, LA 70803

Leo Trich, Jr.
PONY Baseball, Inc.
Washington, PA 15301

5

Coaching Roles
and Relationships

Chapter 1

I'll never forget my first day as a coach. There I was, with a dozen kids looking at me and waiting to be told what to do. I remember thinking, "What do I do now? How did I get myself into this? I know a lot about sports, but I've never coached kids.

Frank L. Smoll, Ronald E. Smith and Bill Curtis
University of Washington

This reaction came from an experienced coach. It is probably fairly common — one you may have experienced. Most coaches know the techniques and strategies of the sport, but are we prepared to deal with kids who look to us to provide a worthwhile and enjoyable experience? Every youngster differs in ability and personality and in the reasons for playing the sport. Some hope to be future champions; some want to have fun; and others are there because their parents or friends have pressured them into participating. There are even those who (perhaps like their coach) wonder what they're doing there. And there you are, trying to meet the needs and expectations of a highly variable group of young personalities. You're a teacher, amateur psychologist, substitute parent, and important role model — in their words, you're a coach!

Many books are available on how to manage a major league baseball team, develop a winning college football team, or teach basketball or soccer skills to high school and college athletes. Most of these focus on developing highly specialized and refined athletic skills and strategies. This chapter will examine the psychological relationships between player and coach, and offer ways you can use this relationship to increase the value of organized sports for your players' personal and social development.

Copyright, 1977, Universal Press Syndicate

Why Kids' Sports?

Estimates of the number of children between the ages of 8 and 16 who are involved in nonschool athletic programs have risen as high as 20 million. Hundreds of thousands of adults like yourself unselfishly give their time and energy to supervise these programs. There can be no doubt that youth sports are an important part of our daily lives and are entrenched in our cultural heritage. In spite of this, the desirability of youth sports has been a topic of controversy and bitter debate.

Those who favor youth sports see them as a medium for desirable psychological development of such positive traits as cooperativeness, ability to work persistently at long-term goals, self-acceptance, achievement motivation, self-assertiveness, respect for others, and the ability to deal with success and failure. Many regard sports as a miniature life situation in which young athletes can learn through winning and losing to cope with realities they will face in later life. Lifelong patterns of physical activity which promote health and fitness also can be established in childhood through sports involvement. Perhaps most important for many kids and adults, sports are just plain fun.

However, there are many critics of organized youth sports. The news media have enthusiastically publicized, sometimes nationally, the criticism that organized youth programs place excessive physical and psychological demands on children. They say youth sports are conducted primarily to satisfy parents and coaches, that children would benefit far more by being left alone to organize their own activities.

Unfortunately, neither side in this youth sports controversy has much solid scientific evidence to support its claims. Both sides frequently use extreme examples to justify their positions. We believe that organized sports are neither universally good nor universally bad for kids. While some of the criticisms are well founded and constructive, we are convinced that sports have tremendous positive potential. Whether this potential is realized depends on how programs are organized and supervised. The issue is not whether kids' sports should exist — they will continue to grow — but rather how to increase the likelihood of a favorable outcome.

That's where coaches come in. We have an important responsibility to the kids to provide competent guidance and instruction in the techniques and strategies of the sport, and to create a psychologically healthy situation in which they can derive the positive benefits of sports participation. By creating such an atmosphere, we can all be winners regardless of our won-lost record. What kids carry away with them will endure far longer than the outcome of a game.

The Many Roles of the Coach

Most of us tend to underestimate the influence we can have on the youngsters who play for us. Many kids are able to hide their true feelings, especially in settings where the traditional "strong athlete" image dominates. But in reality, you play a very prominent role in their lives. Your actions and attitudes help to shape their view of the world and of themselves. For some children, you may be a more important influence than their parents during a formative period of their lives. You enter their world at a time when their normal striving for independence reduces their parents' influence. The youngster may look to you as a substitute for a parent who is missing in either a physical or a psychological sense.

When I was a kid, I had a great coach. He taught me how to bounce back when things were tough. I wish I could thank him now — but I don't even remember his name.

My coach was the one person that I could talk to. Even though I couldn't really discuss the trouble I was having with my folks, my coach was one person who made me feel that someone cared.

I was a puny kid without much talent. But my coach made me feel as if I was better than I thought I could be.

Should this potential impact on a child's life scare you? Not if you have a genuine concern for youngsters and if you have established for yourself what it is you are attempting to accomplish through coaching. Remember, you are not the only adult in a position to exert profound influence on a child. American society entrusts the social, emotional, moral and intellectual development of our children to more sources than just parents and amateur coaches. Teachers, religious leaders and scoutmasters are among those who can take an active role in guiding a child's growth. You as a coach can make an important contribution which, coupled with the contributions of other responsible adults, helps a child on his or her way to a happy, productive and well-adjusted life.

Coaches, like children, involve themselves in sports for many reasons. We must be aware of our goals as coaches, especially when the league has a philosophy underlying its program. Most youth sport programs are oriented toward providing a healthy recreational and social learning experience for kids and are not intended to be miniature professional leagues. Unfortunately, some coaches get caught up in the "winning is everything" philosophy that is so much a part of our sport culture and may temporarily lose sight of what youth coaches should really be about. Coaches should try to build winning teams, but we suspect that often winning becomes more important for the coach than for the players. Our own research has shown that coaches for whom players enjoyed playing most, and who were most successful in promoting feelings of self-worth, actually had won-lost records that were about the same as coaches who were less liked and less effective in fostering feelings of self-worth. Winning will take care of itself within the limits of your players' talents if you work to help the players develop their athletic skills. Such skills are most likely to develop in a positive and happy relationship between you and your players. And while happy players don't always win, they need never lose.

Success as a coach cannot be measured in championship rings and trophies (although some adults may try to make you think so). Even children develop an image of what a coach is supposed to be like. For example, several years ago, we interviewed Little Leaguers shortly after several television specials on Vince Lombardi. Many of the children felt their coaches were inadequate because "they weren't tough enough." We may all wish we could have played for Lombardi's Packers, but not at the age of eight. If kids leave your program having enjoyed relating to you and to their teammates, feeling better about themselves, having improved their skills, and looking forward to further sports participation, you have accomplished something far more important than a winning record or a league championship.

The importance of what you do. All of us (and especially children) learn a great deal by watching and imitating others. Your players will learn as much from what you do as from what you say. Believe it or not, you are a kind of hero to them. They look up to you because you occupy a leadership role in a very significant area of their lives. The way you deal with them and approach problems teaches them to do likewise. For example, if you can't maintain your poise in the face of frustration, how well will your players learn to? If you can't treat officials and umpires with the respect and tolerance they deserve, don't expect your players to act in a dignified manner when calls go against them. Kids are sure to be affected by what you do. In fact, they will remember what you did long after they have forgotten what you said.

The importance of awareness. Each of us is the very best coach we can be, based on our current awareness. Awareness means many things — insight into how we behave and come across to kids and knowledge of how we achieve our goals. Sometimes we may regret things we have done as coaches in the past, but we should remember that we were doing what we thought to be the best thing based on our awareness at that time. Fortunately, awareness can be increased.

The most successful coaches are those who can help each player achieve his or her full potential. The hallmark of such coaches is an awareness of the makeup of each player and the ability to be flexible in approaching each individual. This allows them to do the most effective thing at the most appropriate time.

As a coach, you occupy an important leadership role, and increased awareness can help you increase your effectiveness. The guidelines to follow are based on our experiences as coaches, physical educators and psychologists, as well as on the results of our research on how coaching behaviors affects young athletes. We hope the following will help you increase your awareness and give you a greater ability to provide a valuable athletic and social growth experience for your players.

Relating to Child Athletes: Some Do's and Don'ts

Everybody talks about psychology these days. We hear about the psychology of sex, the psychology of advertising, the psy-

The toughest and most challenging part of coaching is the psychology of getting what you want to teach across to the kids, gaining their respect, and making them feel glad that they played for you. When things click on a psychological level, I find that I really get much more enjoyment out of coaching.

chology of business management and the psychology of sports. Psychology is vitally important because human interaction is essentially people trying to influence each other. As a coach, you are trying to influence children in a number of ways. You want to create a good learning situation. You want to create an enjoyable interpersonal situation where your players relate well to you and each other. You also want to provide a setting or an atmosphere in which your players will develop positive personality traits. Put very simply, you are trying to increase certain desired behaviors on the part of your players and decrease undesirable behaviors.

The psychology of coaching is simply a set of principles to increase the ability to influence others positively. It is often said that psychology is the application of common sense. We think that the following guidelines make good common sense, and they are scientifically valid. The challenge is not so much to learn the principles, but to adapt them to your own coaching style.

There are two basic approaches to influencing people. The *positive approach* is designed to strengthen desirable behaviors by motivating people to perform in a desirable way. The second approach, the *negative approach,* involves attempts to eliminate negative behaviors through punishment and criticism. The motivating factor in the second approach is fear. Both approaches are used by coaches, but the positive approach is preferable. First of all, it works much better! Second, it creates an enjoyable climate.

The importance of reward and encouragement. The positive approach to coaching is characterized by liberal use of *reward* and *encouragement*. The most effective way to build desirable behaviors is to use the "reward power" you have as a coach. In our research, we found that the single most important difference between coaches to whom kids respond most favorably and those to whom they respond least favorably was the frequency with which they rewarded desirable behaviors. Reward can include many things: a pat on the back, a smile, clapping, verbal praise, a friendly nod. Be liberal with reward. Look for positive things, reward them, and you'll see them increase. Praise the little things that others might not notice. Reward, *sincerely* given, does not spoil people; rather, it gives them something to strive for. Have realistic expectations and consistently reward players when they succeed in meeting them. Reward positive things as soon as they occur since immediate reward is more potent. Remember, whether kids show it or not, the positive things you say do stick with them.

What you choose to reward is of critical importance. It's easy to praise a player who just made a great play. It's less natural to reward the player who tried hard but did not make the play. Perhaps the second player deserves reward even more. *Reward effort as much as you do results.* Players have complete control over how much effort they make; they have only limited control over the outcome of their efforts. Don't take these efforts for granted; let the players know that you appreciate and value them. Former UCLA basketball coach John Wooden emphasized this approach in his coaching:

You cannot find a player who ever played for me at UCLA that can tell you that he ever heard me mention "winning" a basketball game. He might say I inferred a little here and there, but I never mentioned winning. Yet the last thing that I told my players, just prior to tipoff, before we would go on the floor was, "When the game

is over, I want your head up — and I know of only one way for your head to be up — and that's for you to know that you did your best . . . This means to do the best YOU can do. That's the best; no one can do more . . . You made that effort.

Encouragement is also an important part of the positive approach to coaching. Most players are already motivated to develop their skills and play well. Encouragement helps to increase their natural enthusiasm. Again, encourage effort; don't demand results. Use encouragement selectively so that it means something. Be supportive without acting like a cheerleader. Never give encouragement in a sarcastic or degrading manner (e.g., "Come on gang, we're only down 37-1. Let's really come back and make it 37-2."); this only irritates and frustrates players.

Be realistic and base your encouragement on reasonable expectations. Don't encourage your eight-year-olds to strive for Olympic standards; they may feel like failures when they can't reach the goals they think you've set. Again, encouraging effort rather than outcome can help avoid this problem.

Encouragement can become contagious and build team unity. It helps communicate your enthusiasm, and this rubs off on your team. Try to get your players to support and encourage each other. The best way to do this is to be an enthusiastic model and to reward your players when they encourage one another (e.g., "Way to go — let's boost each other up!").

As much as we enjoy seeing and reacting to home runs, touchdowns, goals and all-out effort, much of the time coaches must deal with mistakes, screwups, boneheaded plays — all the things that the O.J. Simpsons, Rick Barrys and Joe Morgans seldom do. Your reaction to these situations is critically important. If you handle them wrong, you risk creating a fear of failure in players that can harm their performance and their outlook on themselves, the sport and their coach.

Whether they show it or not, most players feel embarrassed when they make a mistake. The most useful thing you can do is to

give them encouragement immediately after the mistake. That's when the youngster needs it most. If you manage things right, this can also be a golden opportunity to provide *corrective instruction.* The player wishes that he or she had done it correctly, and the instruction may be particularly meaningful at that time. A general principle to follow is: If you are sure the player knows how to correct the mistake, then encouragement alone is sufficient. To tell a player what he or she already knows is more irritating than helpful.

If you feel that it will be useful, give corrective instruction, but in an encouraging and positive fashion. Emphasize not the bad thing that just happened, but the good things that will happen if the player follows your instructions (the "why" of it). Your instruction should have three elements. Start with a *compliment* ("Way to hustle. You really ran a good pattern."). Follow this up with the *future-oriented instruction* ("If you follow the ball all the way into your hands, you'll snag those just like Fred Biletnikof does."). Then, end with another *positive statement* ("Hang in there. You're going to get even better if you work hard at it."). This kind of "sandwich," consisting of a reward for something done right and an encouraging remark wrapped around a constructive suggestion, is apt to make the player feel encouraged as a result of what you've said. Emphasizing the positive things that will happen if he or she follows your instruction will tend to motivate the player to make the good things happen rather than being motivated by avoiding failure and disapproval.

Most of us tend to focus on the negative side of mistakes and regard them as something to be avoided at all costs. But mistakes in fact have a positive side — they provide the information we need to help improve performance and are important stepping stones to achievement. If coaches can communicate this concept to players, they can help them to accept and learn from their mistakes.

There are several "don'ts" to be mentioned in relation to mistakes. Don't punish when things go wrong. Punishing statements ("Let me see the bottom of your feet — I thought so, you're growing roots into the field") do little to increase positive motivation. Punishment isn't just yelling at kids; it can be any form of disapproval, tone of voice or action. Kids respond much better to a positive approach.

Avoid giving corrective instruction in a punitive or hostile manner ("How many times do I have to tell you to catch with two hands? Your teeth will thank you."). This kind of negative approach to giving instructions is more likely to increase frustration and create resentment than to improve performance. Don't let your good intentions in giving instruction be self-defeating.

Athletic motivation takes several forms. Many athletes try to achieve because of a positive desire to succeed. Unfortunately, many others are motivated primarily by fear of failure. The positively motivated athlete welcomes and peaks under pressure, while the youngster who fears failure dreads critical situations and the possibility of failure and disapproval. If he's in the on-deck circle with two outs, his team down by one run and runners on second and third, he's likely to say mentally to the batter, "Either strike out or knock them in, but for Pete's sake, don't walk."

Fear of failure can be an athlete's worst enemy. It harms performance, detracts from the enjoyment of competing, and keeps players from trying, thereby risking failure. Many people fail in their imagination and thus never try.

There are several ways to reduce fear of failure. The positive approach is designed to create positive motivation rather than fear of failing. And if coaches deal honestly and openly with their mistakes, players will be better able to accept their mistakes and learn from them. John Wooden once told a group of coaches:

You must know quite well that you are not perfect, that you're going to make mistakes. But you must not be afraid to act because you're afraid of making mistakes or you won't do anything, and that's the greatest mistake of all. We must have initiative, and act and know that we're going to fail

at times, for failure will only make us stronger if we accept it properly.

Maintaining order and discipline. At a recent coaching clinic, youth coaches discussed common problems. Over two-thirds of their questions had to do with problems of preventing misbehavior during games and practices. This can become a serious problem unless the coach deals with it effectively early in the season.

There are several factors to understand about kids' behaviors in relation to this problem. First, kids are not miniature adults. It is an unusual child who wants to sit still during a vigorous play activity. Pre-adolescents and adolescents are establishing their independence and personal identity, and this can cause them to test the limits imposed by authority figures.

But there is another factor that works in favor of coaches. Kids want clearly defined limits and structure. They don't like unpredictability and inconsistency. Coaches can utilize this desire to create a well-defined situation in which kids can have plenty of freedom and fun within reasonable limits.

There is much evidence that people are more willing to live by rules when (1) they have had a hand in formulating them, and (2) they have made a public commitment to abide by them. While it is your job as coach to maintain reasonable order and discipline, there are several things you can do to involve your players in the process. At older ages, you can introduce the topic at an early team meeting by saying something like: "I think rules and regulations are an important part of the game because the game happens to be rules and regulations. Our team rules ought to be something we can agree upon. I have a set of rules that I feel are important. But we all have to follow them, so you ought to think about what *you* want. They should be your rules too." The advantage of this approach is that if the rules are truly *team* rules, when someone breaks them, it's not the individual versus *your* rules, but the breaking of *their* rules.

Obviously very young children cannot formulate rules; they're looking to you to do that. But even here, players will follow the rules better if they have been involved somehow. When you discuss your rules, make sure the players understand the reason for them and how they'll contribute to making a better team. Ask the players for suggestions and ideas, and *listen* to show that you value their ideas and feelings (although, of course, you don't necessarily accept what you hear as policy).

Formulating rules is easier than dealing with rule violations. The most important thing is to be consistent and impartial. Don't show anger, become punitive, embarrass the players, or lecture. Focus on the fact that they've broken a team policy without degrading them or making them feel they're in your "dog house." Simply remind players that they have violated a rule which they agreed to follow, and because of *that* (not because of *you*) they must automatically pay the penalty. This approach focuses the responsibility where it belongs — on the player — and helps to build a sense of personal accountability and responsibility.

What kinds of penalties should be given out for rules violations? It is best to deprive children of something they value rather than making them do something aversive. For example, telling a player to sit off to the side ("time out") is preferable to making the youngster run laps or do pushups (we don't want beneficial physical activities to become aversive by using them as punishment). Remember also to keep the lines of communication open and alow the child to explain his or her actions. There may be a reasonable cause for what the player did or didn't do.

Rules can play an important role in building team unity. Emphasize that during a game *all* members of the team are part of the game, especially those on the bench. Use reward to strengthen team participation. In other words, apply the positive approach in this area as well. By strengthening desirable behaviors, you can automatically prevent misbehaviors. You know the old saying, "An ounce of prevention . . . " By rewarding players when they're "in the game" and following team rules, you can increase team unity, which is rewarding in itself.

Creating a good learning atmosphere. Your players expect you to help them satisfy their desire to become as skilled as possible. Therefore, establish your role as teacher as early as possible. Try to structure participation as a learning (rather than competitive) situation in which you're going to help the kids develop their abilities.

Always give instruction in a positive manner, emphasizing the good things that will happen if they do it right rather than focusing on the bad things that will occur if they don't. This approach motivates the players to make the good things happen rather than building fear of a mistake. Give instruction in a clear, concise manner and, if possible, show the players how to do it correctly. Reward effort and progress toward the desired performance. Be patient, and don't expect or demand more than maximum effort.

One approach to instruction is to use your more mature and skilled players to instruct younger players. The teacher-learner relationships that develop can help weld the team together, but make sure the player-teachers use the positive approach.

It's important that during each practice or game, every youngster gets recognized at least once. Those players who usually receive the most recognition are the stars or those who are causing problems. The average players need attention as well. When coaches are asked how often they talk to each player, they often discover that there are some players who get very little attention. You might try this yourself.

If an athlete has had a bad practice or a rough game (as we all have), it should not end with the youngster going home feeling badly. The player should get some kind of support from you, a pat on the back, a kind word ("Hey, we're going to work that out in practice," or "This must have been a tough day for you. I know what you're going through, but everyone has days like that sometimes."). Don't let your player leave feeling alienated from you or feeling like a loser.

Gaining players' respect. All of what we've emphasized up to now is relevant to gaining your players' respect. There are two keys to gaining such respect: (1) show your players that you can teach them to develop their skills, and that you're willing to make the effort to do so, and (2) be a fair and considerate leader by showing them that you care about them as individuals and that you're glad to be coaching them.

Set a good example by showing respect for yourself, for them and for others — opponents, parents, officials. You cannot demand respect; it must be earned.

Communicating effectively. Everything you do communicates something to your players. Develop the habit of asking yourself (and, at times, your players) what your actions have communicated, and if you are communicating effectively.

Remember that communication is a two-way street. If you keep the lines of communication open, you will be more aware of opportunities to have a positive impact on players. Fostering two-way communication does not mean that players are free to be disrespectful toward you. Rather, it is an open invitation for players to express their concerns with the assurance that they will be heard by you.

Picture your team as individuals and respond accordingly. For example, a kid who has low self-confidence may be devastated (or very positively affected) by something that has no impact whatever on a youngster with high self-esteem. Be sensitive to the individual needs of your players, and you will be a more successful coach.

Timing is important. You can communicate most effectively when the child is receptive. For example, you may find that one player responds much better to instruction if you wait a while after a mistake; another player may respond best to immediate correction.

A Word about Parents

Parents can indeed create headaches for the coach. Some of them seem to have a greater stake in what's going on than the kids do. We must recognize that the "athletic triangle" consisting of coach, child and parent, is inevitable in youth sports programs. While you may sometimes wish they would stay home, many parents want varying degrees of involvement in the program. You may find it possible in some cases to channel their genuine concerns and good intentions in a way that supports what you're trying to accomplish.

Sometimes parents put excessive pressure on their children. All parents identify with their children to some extent and want them to do well. But for some parents, this identification process goes too far and the child literally becomes an extension of themselves.

Coaching would be so much easier if everything that went on involved only me and the kids. Sometimes I feel that parents forget that this program is run for the kids. They are often more of a problem than the kids. I don't need nine assistant coaches.

When this happens, they begin to define their own self-worth in terms of their child's success. They become "winners" or "losers" through their children. The child *must* succeed or their own self-image is threatened. For such parents, much more is at stake than just a game, and the child of such parents carries a heavy burden.

What can you do as a coach to counteract this tendency? We have already discussed some ways in which the positive approach of encouraging and rewarding *effort* rather than outcome helps to reduce pressure. By communicating to your players that the important thing is that they enjoy playing and develop their skills, not that they must win, you can help them develop a more desirable attitude toward participation. If you can get the parents to understand and reinforce this approach, you can benefit both the player and the parent. It may be important to communicate openly to some parents that excessive pressure on the kids can detract from the potential that youth sports can have for enjoyment and personal growth.

Copyright 1976 Universal Press Syndicate

Some coaches have found it useful to have a meeting with parents before the season to discuss this issue. If we can get the parents working as part of a team trying to achieve a common goal, we can reduce the chances that misunderstandings will result in problems. Here are some topics that could be covered at such a meeting:

1. Your appreciation of their interest and concern
2. The goals of the program
3. The specific approach you plan to use. (A description of the positive approach and why you favor it may actually teach the parents some useful principles that they can apply in relating to their children.)
4. How they as parents can assist in attainment of the program's goals
5. Your willingness to discuss with them any problems that might arise.

Sometimes parents will disagree with what you're doing. Perhaps they won't like the fact that you seem incapable of recognizing the latent superstar abilities of their child. Or maybe they know the *right* way of teaching kids how to catch fly balls. The main thing is not to get defensive. Listen to what they have to say even if you don't agree. You can afford at least to do this while recognizing that *you* are the coach and have the final say. You may find some of the suggestions useful. But also remember that no coach can please everyone, and no one can ask any more of you than that you be the best coach you can be.

A Final Word

As a coach, you are giving a great deal of time and energy to provide a worthwhile life experience for children. By putting to use the basic principles presented above, you can enhance the positive impact you have on young people's lives. Don't underestimate your importance in the personal and athletic growth of your players, or the extent to which your efforts are appreciated. Strive to make the experience as much fun and as personally meaningful for the average- and low-ability player as for the superstar. You will have a lot of fun in the process.

Characteristics of the Young Athlete

Chapter 2

G. Lawrence Rarick
University of California — Berkeley
and
Vern Seefeldt
Michigan State University

The first chapter described the role model that coaches of young athletes must assume, their commitments, and the sensitivity they must have for the feelings of the young athlete during moments of success and periods of frustration. This chapter deals with the young athlete's growth characteristics. Between the ages of 8 to 18 years, there are marked changes in general body size and dimensions, and organ and tissue development. There are also somewhat parallel gains in the individual's functional capabilities, i.e., strength and power, endurance, coordination and intellectual function.

It is important for the coach to be thoroughly acquainted with the growth characteristics of the age group with which he or she is working, to have a realistic outlook on the performance capabilities and limitations which age, maturational level and body structure are likely to impose. Such information is valuable in setting up training regimens that attain the most effective results and give young athletes the protection they must have.

PHYSICAL DEVELOPMENT

1. Characteristics of Growth

The rate at which we achieve maturity is an individual process; for example, infants at birth have nearly one-fourth of their total body length and continue to have tremendous changes in height, weight and shape in the following two or three years. Growth is more modest and stable during the middle and late childhood years, followed by the "adolescent spurt," and then a negative acceleration that completes the growth cycle.

The rates of human growth in standing height are shown in Figure 1.

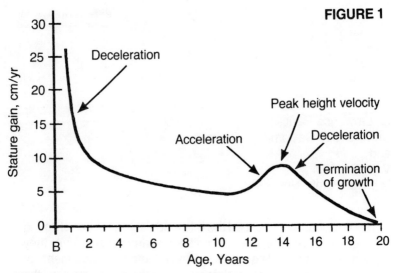

Figure 1. The human curve for standing height showing rapid, modest and slow periods of growth. From R. Malina, *Growth and Development: The First Twenty Years In Man* (Minneapolis: Burgess, 1975), p.21.

Similar patterns occur in all body segments, organs and tissues, with positive and negative accelerations at differing ages for males and females.

FIGURE 2

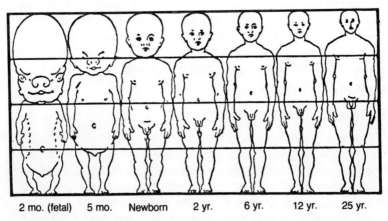

Figure 2. Growth of the head, trunk, arms and legs at various ages. From E. Watson and G. Lowrey, *Growth and Development of Children* (Chicago: Year Book Medical Publishers, 1962), p.44.

Although growth is a continuous process, there are certain body segments that are further from their final size at birth, and hence have an accelerated overall growth, while others change their rates of growth several times between birth and maturity. Figure 2 shows the percent of total body length comprised by the various segments as the individual grows from a fetus to an adult.

In Figure 2 the head takes up approximately one-half of the total body length during early intrauterine life, but only about 15 percent of the total height at adulthood. Conversely, the legs comprise less than 20 perenct of the total body length during the second fetal month, and approximately 50 percent of the total standing height in the mature adult.

A comparison of growth rates from birth to maturity reveals that some segments of the body are closer to their final size at birth than others. The various segmental dimensions of the newborn child, compared to the mature adult, are illustrated in Figure 3.

FIGURE 3

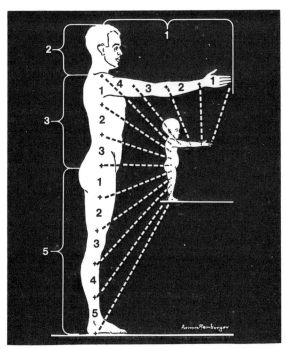

Figure 3. Proportional growth of the body segments from birth to adulthood. From W. Krogman, "The Physical Growth of Children: An Appraisal of Studies, 1950-1955", *Mono. Soc. Res. Child Devel.,* vol, 20, no. 26, 1955, p.3.

Note that the head at birth is 50 percent of its adult size, while the trunk trebles, the upper extremities quadruple and the lower extremities increase five-fold at adult size. The legs and arms undergo greater increases than any of the other segments during the growing years.

The changes in segmental size and shape occur at varying times in the process toward maturity. The changing body proportions, with their commensurate developmental ages, are shown in Figure 4.

────────────────────────────────────FIGURE 4

CHANGING BODILY PROPORTIONS

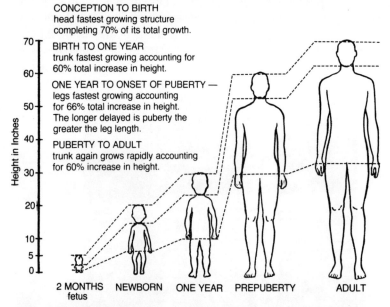

Figure 4. Changing body proportions from conception to adulthood. From D. Whipple, *Dynamics of Development: Euthenic Pediatrics.* (New York: McGraw-Hill, 1966), p.122. Used with permission of McGraw-Hill.

The time between one year and prepuberty is marked by accelerated growth of the arms and legs. Children about to enter puberty commonly are described as consisting of "all arms and legs." Generally, this disproportionate length of the extremities to the remainder of the body is a temporary situation, halted when the epiphyses and the long bones fuse. Since the internal structures of the arms and legs cease their growth with epiphyseal fusion, the trunk has a continued opportunity to grow after the long bones have reached their mature size. Thus, the mature proportions of the adult are acquired late in the growing process.

2. Maturational Differences in Body Type

Different abilities among young athletes are often a result of different maturational levels, even though the boys or girls being compared may be of the same chronological age. An example of such a dissimilarity in maturational level is shown in Figure 5.

FIGURE 5

Age 13 yr.　　　　　　　　　　　　　　　　　　　　　**13 yr.**
1 mo.

Figure 5. Children of the same age but of differing levels of maturity. From D. Whipple, *Dynamics of Development: Euthenic Pediatrics* (New York: McGraw-Hill, 1966), p. 128.

The two boys are about the same chronological age, yet one has the build of a mature adult and the other resembles a child four or five years from physical maturity. It is not unusual for differences in rate of maturity to exceed five years within one chronological age. A group of 12-year-old boys or girls will customarily include individuals whose body cells are not yet at the maturity level of the average 10-year-old, while others will have maturational ages equivalent to 15 chronological years.

The rate at which children mature is closely related to their body size. The three usual classifications of body shapes are shown in Figure 6.

FIGURE 6

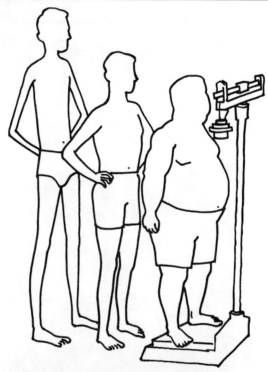

Figure 6. The three varieties of physique, showing ectomorphic, mesomorphic and endomorphic body builds. From D. Whipple, *Dynamics of Development: Euthenic Pediatrics* (New York: Mc-Graw-Hill, 1966), p.36. Used with permission of McGraw-Hill.

The individual on the left has a linear body and is classified as an "ectomorph." Individuals with linear bodies generally mature at a slower rate than others of the same age and sex, but have greater proportions of muscle and bone. Mesomorphs are exemplified by the individual in the middle, and endomorphs have an abundance of fat and viseral tissue.

During childhood, endomorphic and mesomorphic body types are likely to be the tallest and heaviest individuals within any chronological age group. They mature at an earlier age and therefore tend to be shorter and have a stockier body build as adults, compared to the later maturing individuals with an ecto-morphic (linear) body build.

3. Growth and Maturational Differences in Boys and Girls

At birth boys tend to be slightly longer and heavier than girls, but this difference soon disappears. There is no significant difference in the heights and weights of males and females during the childhood years. However, girls are nearer their final body size at any age because they mature faster than boys. For example, at six years the body cells of girls are nearly a full year closer to maturity than those of boys. By 14 years, girls are two full years ahead of males biologically. At 15, most girls have reached their final stature, while most boys do not complete their growth until 17.

Typical growth curves for height and weight of males and females are shown in Figure 7.

━━━━━━━━━━━━━━━━━━━━━━━━━━━━**FIGURE 7**

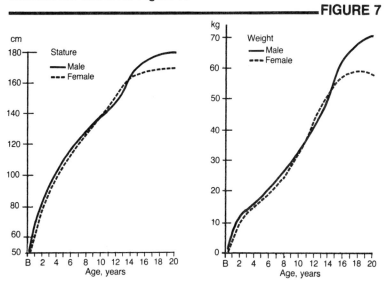

Figure 7. Distance curves for height, showing the adolescent spurt of males and females. From R. Malina, *Growth and Development: The First Twenty Years In Man* (Minneapolis: Burgess, 1975), p. 19.

Curves for height and weight for both sexes follow the same basic pattern; the first several years are marked by rapid but negatively accelerating growth, modest and stable growth during middle and late childhood, followed by the adolescent growth spurt, when growth doubles or triples its previous rate. After the peak velocity in height is reached, there is a negative acceleration for two or three years until growth finally ceases. A comparison of the ages when the rapid and slower growth rates occur in boys and girls is shown in Figure 8.

FIGURE 8

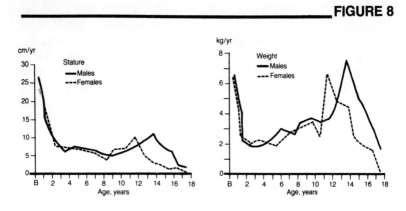

Figure 8. Velocity curves for height and weight of males and females. From R. Malina, *Growth and Development: The First Twenty Years In Man* (Minneapolis: Burgess, 1975), p.20

Most of the characteristic differences in the skeletal structure of boys and girls appear during the adolescent spurt, when boys surpass the girls in standing height and weight (see Figure 7.) The arms and legs of post-pubescent boys are longer than those of girls because of a longer period of growth at the normal rate, in addition to a more intense growth spurt.

The characteristic differences in body shape and size between males and females appear at puberty, with (1) the broadening of shoulders in relation to relatively little growth in the hips of males and (2) the increased growth in the hip width of females in relation to relatively little gain in shoulder width. These changes in breadth and circumferences are the result of tissue responses to hormones secreted by the testes and ovaries as they mature.

4. Development of Muscle, Bone, Fat

Sex differences in muscle, bone and fat are small at birth, but become more distinct as age advances. Males have a greater body density than females at birth as a result of their greater muscle mass, while females have greater amounts of fatty tissue. The sex differences in muscle, bone and fat become greater during adolescence when the male hormone, testosterone, helps build muscle tissue, while in females, estrogen promotes the accumulation of fat about the hips, breasts and buttocks. During adolescence, the male skeleton also becomes larger and denser than the female's.

5. Influence of Exercise on Growth and Maturation

"How will this training program affect the way my child grows?" "Are the goals of the coach in the best interest of my child?" These questions are asked countless times each year by parents of children who face new or changing competitive situations. There is no single answer because the influence of exercise on growth and maturation depends on: the intensity and duration of the activity and the developmental level of the child. Exercise can be both beneficial and detrimental to physical growth, depending upon the conditions under which it takes place.

Muscles, bones and nervous tissue must be subjected to activity if they are to reach their potential for development. Conversely prolonged bed rest or immobilization of a limb in a cast will result in atrophy of muscle tissue and depletion of the mineral stores in bone. These general statements concerning the role of exercise on growth avoid answering the question, How much activity and what specific types should children have to grow properly? This question has not been answered and probably never will be because we do not know what activities, in what amounts, are essential for growing children. However, experience and research have provided some guidelines that may be helpful to coaches who have the responsibility of supervising activities for young athletes.

It is doubtful whether training programs for most youthful performers, on a competitive basis, have any influence on their height or linear growth. Studies on young swimmers and runners reveal that they grew slightly more than children of the same age and sex who did not engage in these activities. Conversely, other studies have shown that young wrestlers and basketball players had reduced rates of growth as a result of taking part in lengthy, highly competitive seasons. The repetitive act of throwing a baseball has been shown to increase the rate of maturation of the throwing arm, causing marked changes in the elbow joint at the point where the greatest stress was applied. It is safe to conclude that any repetitive activity that results in discomfort to the exercised body part is a source of undue stress, while moderate stress in the form of exercises found in many youth sports programs can be a positive force in bone growth.

The most notable effects of exercise occur in muscle and adipose tissue. Muscle cells enlarge (undergo hypertrophy) as a result of stress. The increase in size is directly related to the intensity and duration of the training program. However, attempts to build muscle mass in young athletes through weight training or other heavy resistance exercises are questionable because of the inefficiency of increasing muscle tissue prior to puberty and the possible detrimental effects that overloading the joints may have on the ends of the long bones.

The most dramatic effects are the loss of adpose tissue. Energy expenditure beyond that which is replaced daily through food will result in a reduction of fatty tissue. The use of activity to control weight is an important side effect of youth sports programs since much adult obesity is the result of poor dietary and exercise patterns during childhood.

PHYSIOLOGICAL DEVELOPMENT

Since many youth sports involve rather high levels of physical activity, it is important that those supervising youth sports know something about the physiological adjustments the body makes to exercise.

The human body is well equipped by nature to respond to the stresses of diseases, injury and exercise. Such responses are essentially of two kinds — those which occur almost immediately and those adaptations in structure and function which the body makes over relatively long periods of time. The more readily discernible initial adjustments to disease are fever, increases in heart rate and faster and deeper breathing. The long-range response may be development of immunity to the specific disease. The response to injury may be localized swelling at the site of injury, followed by the laying down of repair tissue. The body also responds immediately and effectively to exercise to maintain its dynamic equilibrium. Rapid and deep breathing, pounding heart, flushed skin, and sweating are obvious reactions to the stress of exercise. The more lasting effects of regular exercise result in adaptations in structure and function which normally permit individuals to respond to the exercise with greater ease and permit them to tolerate work loads that would have been impossible otherwise. Let's examine the adjustments and adaptations the human body makes to the stress of physical activity. *These factors are presented here because of their immediate relationships to growth and development. Each factor is treated in more detail in subsequent chapters in this book. (Editor's note).*

1. Adjustments to Exercise

a. Cardiorespiratory adjustments. The degree to which the human body expends energy depends on the intensity and duration of the exercise. To meet these energy requirements, the muscle cells need fuel (free fatty acids and glycogen) and oxygen from the bloodstream. Since the oxygen supply of the muscle cells is rapidly depleted (much more rapidly than the fuel), the respiratory and circulatory systems provide a steady flow of oxygen to the muscles. This means that during intensive exercise, the frequency and depth of breathing must be increased to keep the blood supplied with oxygen. Similarly, the flow of blood to the muscles must be increased by raising the heart rate and correspondingly, the amount of blood ejected at each heart beat. As a rule of thumb it can be said that both pulmonary ventilation and cardiac output vary directly with the intensity of the exercise until it reaches a level when the oxygen requirements of the working muscles can no longer be met. Beyond this point, physical activity can be continued for only a brief period. The foregoing is true in the age range 8 to 18 years for both sexes, regardless of the state of training. Cardiorespiratory adjustments are perhaps the most dramatic and readily discernible ones the body makes to the demands of exercise.

Coaches should be aware that the working capacity of the young child is substantially less than that of adolescents. Allowing for body size, the child 8 to 10 years of age can supply only 80 percent as much oxygen to the working muscles as the adolescent of 16 to 18 years.

b. Temperature adjustments. Much of the energy developed by the muscles during exercise is heat which must be dissipated if work is to continue. Some of the heat is lost through breathing, but most of it is lost through the skin by radiation, conduction and evaporation of sweat. In heavy exercise, the blood flow to the skin increases, which helps dissipate heat by conduction and radiation.

When the air is hot and dry, heat loss occurs primarily by evaporation of sweat. The water lost in sweating must be replaced during exercise by equivalent amounts of water. Failure to do this may produce a drop in blood volume and an excessive rise in body temperature, reducing the effectiveness of the athlete's performance. If water loss is carried to the extreme, it can have disastrous results. The temperature control mechanism in children is sensitive to stress, thus they should not be allowed to engage in heavy exercise in hot, humid conditions.

2. Adaptations to Exercise

Perhaps the most striking functional adaptations associated wth training occur in the neuromuscular system and the heart.

a. Neuromuscular system. Muscles become stronger when exercised and tend to lose their strength when training stops. What is not as well known is that the response capabilities of muscles depend to a considerable degree upon the type of training. In isometric training (exerting muscular force against a fixed resistance), the ability to exert muscular force is increased, but there may be little improvement in muscular endurance or in the power to move a load with speed. In other words, the kind of strength that is developed tends to be closely associated with the training procedures. Conventional weight training programs will not necessarily develop muscular endurance nor are they likely to add much to the speed of movement.

Overload, or placing more than the normal demands on the muscles, will, over a period of time, gradually increase their response capabilities. Thus, overload training involves increasing the load to be moved or the number of repetitions, or both. The coach of the young athlete must clearly understand the kind of strength the sport requires and use strengthening exercises that simulate the movements required in the sport. If a high degree of isometric strength is desired, the number of repetitions should be kept low, and the weight should be 75 to 80 percent of the maximum strength.

Children and adolescents respond positively to muscle strengthening activities. In general, children are adapted to a lower level of strength utilization than adults and hence show substantial training effects. Studies have shown that the greatest response to strength training is between the ages of 12 to 15. This is probably because of the impact of sexual maturation on the growth of muscle tissue, particularly in the male. Marked strength gains during the adolescent growth spurt are characteristic of both males and females, although in early adolescence the gains in strength lag well behind the increases in body size. Athletes in early adolescence may not be as strong as their size would suggest.

On the average, boys are stronger than girls at all ages from 8 to 18 years. Prior to puberty, the differences are not great and are probably more the result of the males' greater physical activity than sex differences, as such. After 13 years of age, males show a marked spurt in strength development, much greater than that of females. The gain made by males at puberty is associated with an increased production of androgens (concomitant with sexual maturity) and its positive influence on muscular development. Female sexual maturity results in limited production of androgens and hence slight gains in muscularity. Allowing for body size, the strength of adolescent females is approximately 80 percent of that of males, with the male having substantially higher potential for strength development.

The age increases in muscular power, reflected by improved performance in running and jumping activities, are substantially greater than one might predict from age increases in body size. The rate of gain is, in fact, greater than that made in the isometric strength of the muscles responsible for these movements. This means that with advancing age, the body is apparently more able to mobilize and utilize the available muscle strength through the improved muscle coordination that comes from experience.

b. The heart. The heart is a muscle that responds to physical training in much the same way as body musculature. Studies of animals have shown that the heart, as a result of heavy training increases in size and its contractile power is enhanced markedly. The stroke volume is increased by training, which produces a greater cardiac output and hence a greater capacity for aerobic work. Studies on adolescent male and female athletes have clearly shown that endurance training creates an increased functional capability of the heart. Less is known about the effects of strenuous training on the heart of the pre-pubescent athlete. Distance running is being used in some localities with children under 12 years of age with apparently no harmful effects, but it is too early to know what the long-range impact of this kind of activity will be on their health.

3. Exercise Tolerance

The body's ability to handle the stress of heavy exercise is not as great in the young athlete as in the more mature adolescent. This is not only a reflection of body size, but of the general immaturity of the skeletal, muscular, cardiovascular and nervous systems of the child. In other words, the athlete of 8 to 12 years is not a miniature adult. Even so, the exercise tolerance of healthy children in this age range is greater than is generally realized. A popular concern is that endurance-type competitive sports may put excessive demands on the hearts of children and early adolescents. Cardiologists now agree that the heart of the growing child is able to respond to the demands of heavy exercise with no evidence that the normal heart is damaged by such stress. There is enough research to indicate that children respond favorably to endurance-type training, provided that careful medical screening and judicious training procedures are followed. We must remember that there have been cases of cardiac arrest and sudden death in young athletes. Autopsies in such cases usually reveal a history of cardiac problems in the family or earlier cardiac difficulties that have either been incorrectly diagnosed or ignored.

4. Hazards of Stressful Activity

Perhaps the greatest concern for the physical well being of youth engaging in stressful competitive sports is the vulnerability of the immature skeleton to irreparable injury. The growing ends of the long bones (epiphyses or growth plates) in the immature skeleton are particularly vulnerable to continuous heavy pressure, to blows and to sudden wrenching. Such stresses, if severe, may derange the normal process of bone growth and result in permanent damage. There may be fragmentation of the growth plate, and, if untreated, it could result in the formation of calcified necrotic bone, thus limiting free mobility of the joint. During the early stages of such injuries, the symptoms of pain, such as tenderness over the epiphysis, reduced range of motion and occasional muscle spasms, may be slight. The healing process extends over several months or even years during which the ossification centers may become compressed and at times deformed. Such a condition is called "traumatic epiphysitis" and is usually related to a single traumatic experience or to repeated stresses on the growth plate.

Weight-bearing activities such as running on a hard, unyielding surface or landing with the knees fully extended, place undue stress on the epiphyses of the lower extremities. "Little Leaguers' elbow," so named because it is occasionally seen in young baseball pitchers, may be brought on by repeated stress on the elbow (medial epicondyle of the humerus) from the powerful contractions of arm muscles used in throwing. There would seem to be little question that these structures are particularly vulnerable to injury in the age range 8 to 14 years. Little League recognizes this danger and hence restricts a boy or girl to no more than six innings of pitching per week, and if the child pitches more than three innings in a day there must be three days rest before pitching is again permitted. There is serious question regarding the advisability of players under 14 years of age using curve ball pitching. It should be added that the frequency of epiphyseal injury is less than two percent in ages under 15 years. Such injuries, if treated immediately and properly, are not apt to result in permanent damage. The probability of permanent damage depends on the type and severity of the epiphyseal injury and the age at which it occurs. The probability of deformity decreases with older children where ossification of the growth centers is almost complete, while the young child with many years of growth remaining, is more vulnerable to repetitive stressful movements. Cuts, lacerations, bruises and sprains can be expected in youth sports programs, but such injuries, if properly treated, are not likely to impair the normal processes of growth.

The best insurance against epiphyseal injury is a judicious decision regarding appropriate sports for those under 14 years, proper conditioning and protective equipment. Collision sports such as tackle football and ice hockey are suspect, as are activities in which there is continuous heavy pounding or undue pressure on the growing ends of long bones.

5. Common Myths and Misunderstandings

There are many misconceptions about exercise that may influence the procedures to be followed in preparing young athletes for competition. Many believe that special foods and diets will enhance the athlete's performance. Extensive research has been conducted on dietary supplements such as gelatin, dextrose, salt, sugar and vitamins, as well as high protein diets. There is little, if any, evidence to indicate that any of the foregoing, when used in conjunction with nutritious well-balanced diets, will enhance the strength or performance of athletes, training effects aside. Amphetamine, a powerful and dangerous drug, has been used in experiments on the endurance of athletes, but in the dosages employed, its effects have not been significant.

Anabolic steroids have been used with mature athletes, and

gains in muscle mass and muscular strength have been reported but in general these studies lack acceptable experimental control. The hazardous side effects of using anabolic steroids are widely recognized, and no reputable physician or coach would recommend their use by young athletes.

The value of extensive warm-ups prior to competition remains a controversial question, one that has not yet been proven, as is the practice of special meals immediately prior to competition. Coaches should accept what research has established — that there is no safe and effective substitute for a good conditioning program, one that is oriented to the event for which the athlete is training.

PSYCHOLOGICAL CONSIDERATIONS

1. Interest Versus Effort

The urge to be physically active is so strong in the young that healthy children normally enter into active childhood games without adult direction. In the eyes of the child, there are very real differences between work and play, and they are likely to regard highly structured training programs as work regardless of the inducements.

With the approach of adolescence, there comes a need for group membership, accompanied by a yearning for peer approval. There is a strong need for adolescents to prove themselves in activities popular within their social group. For many, competitive sports satisfy this need and many adolescents are eager to commit themselves to training programs that demand time and effort.

In the age range 8 to 10 there is little advantage in providing structured training regimens. It is only with the exceptionally talented and highly motivated that much is accomplished prior to 12 or 13 years of age. The wise coach who trains adolescents should recognize that training sessions must be varied to keep motivation high, particularly to avoid practices that emphasize effort and overlook interest.

2. Readiness for Stressful Situations

Psychological stress in sports is usually created by fear, real or imaginary, from concern for physical safety to haunting doubts about future levels of performance. Whatever the cause, it generates nervous tension, and, under extreme conditions, deterioration in neuromuscular skill. For many athletes, moderate psychological stress serves as a stimulus, setting the stage for high level performance. The coach of the young athlete should realize that individuals differ markedly in their ability to cope with stressful situations; some respond with poise and emotional balance, others with diminished judgement and skill.

The less mature and less experienced the athletes, the more sensitive they are likely to be to stressful stuations. Inducing strong psychological stress in young athletes to enhance performance is not apt to succeed, and at best is a questionable practice.

Stressful situations are most effectively met by full understanding of the situation and confidence in one's ability to handle it. Coaches can do much to prepare young athletes for what might be stressful situations by maintaining a low profile themselves, by developing in their athletes a balanced attitude toward winning and losing, and by engendering a confidence justified by their capabilities.

3. Perceptual Development

At eight years of age the normal child has a broad repertoire of motor skills upon which to draw. Refinements in the movement patterns underlying these skills come with maturation and practice. New skills are developed by modifying and combining already established movement patterns in ways that approximate the demands of new tasks. Such processes are highly involved and not entirely understood, but it is clear that the central nervous system must process information of several kinds for motor responses to be effective. Information from the environment (usually visual cues), sensations from muscles, tendons, joints and the center of balance, and recollection of movements used under similar circumstances must be meaningfully processed so that new movements will meet the demands of the task.

It is often said that individuals learn by their mistakes. This is true, for an important aspect of acquiring motor skills is the way the central nervous system handles information on errors and the motor planning that takes place to correct the faulty movements. There must be a conscious effort to integrate the various sources of information properly in anticipation of the next effort. Performance errors may be partially corrected by self-help, but this in no way guarantees that the movements employed will provide the desired level of performance. Young athletes may know when their performance has been faulty, but they need specific coaching direction (verbal or demonstration) to correct their mistakes. Appropriate help will also reduce the trial and error approach and provide some guarantee that the young athlete will acquire the movements best suited to the task.

KINESIOLOGICAL CONSIDERATIONS

1. General Age and Sex Changes in Motor Performance

The ability to perform skills that require strength, power, endurance and total body coordination generally increases during the childhood years. Performance measures for females tend to stabilize at puberty; males show a steady increase of proficiency into adulthood. The ability of young athletes to increase their skill level is directly related to the growth of muscle tissue and the amount of time that is devoted to practice of the motor skills involved. The specific reasons for the decrease in the overall performance of females at puberty and beyond are unknown, but their increased difficulty in maintaining muscle mass after puberty appears to be a primary factor in lowered performance.

2. Biomechanical Considerations of Age, Sex and Body Build

The increased ability of children to perform motor skills more successfully as they mature is due to their change in body size. Longer levers, accompanied by greater muscle mass, will result in greater force if the force is applied correctly. As stated earlier, athletes with a mesomorphic body build tend to mature earlier than those with ectomorphic body builds. The combination of physical attributes and a more mature central nervous system gives the mesomorph an advantage in athletic competition.

Differences in performance levels between males and females are partially due to changes that occur at puberty in body structure. After puberty, the male skeleton is larger, more dense and possesses longer levers than that of the female. Other structural differences that may influence performance levels are a more stable pelvic structure and a more oblique pelvic-humeral articulation in the female. Theoretically, these sex-linked characteristics could limit the degree of pelvic rotation in such skills as throwing and striking. The oblique pelvic-femoral articulation could also cause the advancing thigh to cross the midline in running, resulting in a "knock-kneed" gait.

The greatest differences between performance levels of males and females occur in skills involving force production by the upper extremities. The smaller, less dense shoulder girdle of the female, in combination with a smaller muscle mass acting on a shorter lever, contributes to the skill level differences between the sexes. In addition, the greater carrying angle of the female upper extremity may inhibit the ability to transfer the force of the rotating joints to the object that is to be projected.

Theoretically, the earlier age of maturity in females should provide an advantage over the later-maturing males in skills that demand agility, balance and total body coordination. In reality, most of the sports skills combine the above components with strength, power and endurance. Thus, the greater muscle mass of the male serves to cancel the maturational advantage of the female.

BILL OF RIGHTS FOR YOUNG ATHLETES

The popularity of competitive sports for children does not mean that the programs are free of controversy. One of the most frequent criticisms of youth sports programs is that they are organized by adults — for adults. While such criticisms may be justified in specific situations, the foundation of competitive programs for children is the adult leadership provided by volunteer coaches and officials. Although the motives of adults who supervise children sports programs may be sound, the programs do not always provide safe, beneficial and satisfying experiences for the young participants.

The following "Bill of Rights for Young Athletes," written in an attempt to protect young athletes from adult exploitation, was written by medical, physical education and recreation experts. The 10 "Rights" are directed at coaches, leaders of recreation programs, officials and parents in the hope that their implementation will provide the beneficial effects of athletic competition to all participants.

Bill of Rights for Young Athletes

1. Right of the opportunity to participate in sports regardless of ability level

2. Right to participate at a level that is commensurate with each child's developmental level

3. Right to have qualified adult leadership

4. Right to participate in safe and healthy environments

5. Right of each child to share in the leadership and decision-making of their sport participation

6. Right to play as a child and not as an adult

7. Right to proper preparation for participation in the sport

8. Right to an equal opportunity to strive for success

9. Right to be treated with dignity by all involved

10. Right to have fun through sport

Different Strokes for Different Folks: Teaching Skills to Kids

Chapter 3

Robert N. Singer
Florida State University

Children often have a greater capability than expected to do well in a variety of athletic events. The involvement and challenge of sports competition can produce motivation to achievement, enjoyment, self-fulfillment and improved skills if the athletic experience is conducted by knowledgeable and sensitive coaches.

How can we determine performance and learning potential? How are children similar and how are they different in responding to instructional approaches? Remember that youngsters come to your program with different backgrounds, expectations, motivations and capabilities. Certain approaches to coaching should be effective for most of the participants in your program, but always be ready to use alternatives when appropriate.

In many ways, children should be considered in the same way as any beginning learners. The learning of specific sports skills will be hindered:

1. the more the child is developmentally immature

2. the more difficult the activity is for the youngster's capabilities

3. the more restricted the child's previous experiences have been in a wide range of movement patterns related to the success in the specialized skills associated with a sport.

With consideration of these factors, let us remember that

1. Activities should be modified to the appropriate maturational level, including playing rules, equipment and facilities.

2. Children should be encouraged to develop fundamental movement patterns prior to specialized sports skills training.

Assuming the young athlete is ready in terms of development, past experiences and attitude to acquire specialized sports skills, we can now turn to the most favorable ways of promoting the learning experience.

GENERAL COACHING TIPS

1. Think of your problems in learning new skills. Children have similar ones. Be understanding and patient.

Charles M. Schulz

2. Children have different motives for participating on a team; some play because their parents encouraged or forced them, some want to learn skills and enjoy participation, others need to demonstrate excellence at something, others may have different motives. Be alert and sensitive to various reasons, they will be reflected in motivation to learn and to persevere and in receptivity to instructions.

3. Be positive in your approach. Try to develop a positive self-concept in the young athletes. Encourage, don't discourage.

4. Training can be hard and boring. Why not find ways for the kids to have fun at the same time?

The Child's Capabilities

With age and maturation, the child develops greater capabilities to accomplish the challenging activities provided in sport. Realize that performance is based on the integration of a number of processes and functions, mainly:

> **1.** receiving information
> **2.** making sense of information and decision making
> **3.** responding
> **4.** using feedback

Receiving information. The aspiring athlete can obtain information of what is expected through many possible sources. Learning disabilities can impair learning and performance.

Making sense of information and decision making. A youngster can only handle a limited amount of information at any given

---

Overloading the System

time. Too much in the way of cues, advice or directions can be confusing, frustrating and wasteful. Too little may also be a waste of time and bore the athlete.

Attention span and the ability to concentrate develop with maturation, experience and learning, as does the ability to respond to the most important cues in the situation. Such is the case with making quick and correct decisions in events where it is necessary. The mental processes associated with the learning and performance of athletic skills are often taken for granted. Yet, a careful analysis of the demands of sport suggests that mental processes are involved in a variety of ways, such as getting the idea of what is to be done, concentrating on the minimum and most relevant cues, making rapid and appropriate decisions, and using feedback to improve future performances.

The Act of Concentration

Responding. The easiest process you can analyze is associated with physical movements. Is the athlete performing correctly? Realize that the performance observed is a function of mental processes, appropriate motivation level, and the presence of the ability to time movements appropriately in space (muscular integration). If the athletic performance is not effective, it can be because of a number of reasons.

Using feedback. The athlete can receive information as to the nature of his/her performance both during and after the activity if the movements are slow enough. This feedback can be obtained from one's own efforts or from another person.

The ultimate objective is to help the young athlete become more self-evaluative and self-dependent. With proper guidance, more information can be derived from one's own performance and used to enhance subsequent performances.

Analyzing Athletic Activities

Activities may be categorized in different ways, depending upon the demands placed on the athlete. Two such classifications are *self-paced* and *externally paced* activities, which suggest alternative approaches to coaching.

Self-paced activities allow the athlete to begin when ready and move at his or her own pace, such as in hitting a golf ball, rolling a bowling ball, serving a tennis ball and shooting a foul shot.

Externally paced activities require the athlete to respond quickly to sudden and unpredictable cues. Fast decision making and adaptive behaviors are usually associated with skilled performance in externally-paced activities. Competition in tennis, football, hockey and many sports contains such situations.

In self-paced activities, there is a greater emphasis on attaining consistency in performance. Practice is usually fairly repetitive. Many externally paced activities should probably be learned initially under the more controlled self-paced conditions. Ultimately, practice in externally paced activities should encourage familiarization with many situations. Young athletes need to learn how to anticipate, make rapid decisions and demonstrate appropriate adjustments to the situations. They have to learn how to think!

Getting the Idea

Regardless of the nature of the activity, you must decide on some technique for communicating to the athletes what they are expected to accomplish. Live demonstrations, films, illustrations, and written or verbal words are typical. Some recommendations are:

1. Learners must have a clear idea what it is they are trying to accomplish.

2. Keep the orientation process simple.

3. Observation and modeling techniques should be used, especially with younger athletes.

4. Have the attention and interest of the athletes.

5. Have the athletes optimally motivated to learn (too much is deteriorating and too little results in boredom and inattention).

6. Have athletes learn how to evaluate their present capabilities so they can assess personal improvement and establish realistic objectives for themselves.

7. Analyze the activities to be learned very carefully, along with the skill level of the athletes so that reasonable and attainable goals are established.

General Practice Considerations

Children are restless and active. They can only handle so much information at one time. Your challenge is to offer adequate guidance and then get as many of the athletes as possible immersed in the activity. Progress will be determined by the capabilities and motivations of the athletes as well as your instructional techniques and communication style.

Let us identify some common problems, regardless of type of sports, and suggest what can be done to resolve them. You are continually faced with a series of decisions. In many ways, they result in trade-offs. You may gain one thing but lose something else as you make a decision.

Communication. Be clear in what you want your athletes to do. When directions and cues are provided, the athlete has to learn how to associate verbal labels for the expected movements. Don't assume that the young athlete has already made that association. The adult vocabulary is not the same as a child's.

© King Features Syndicate, Inc. 1977

Developmental as well as cultural factors must be considered. Jargon and speech patterns, which may be ethnic or racial, need to be understood if communication between the coach and athletes is to be effective.

Fun. Why not make learning situations enjoyable as well as productive? Learning drills can be made into games. Children won't look forward to practice if the program is rigid and formal. Adults have learned to discipline themselves in order to work hard to attain goals; children have not.

When practice sessions are more interesting, young athletes will be more inclined to go to practice and learn skills over a longer period of time. You should develop a variety of learning games to maintain a high level of enthusiasm and keep the athletes active.

Learning to think. The easiest way to coach is continually to direct the activities of the athletes. Formal, prescribed learning techniques promote the making of associations. The athletes are conditioned to follow orders. Guidance is obviously necessary for learning purposes as well as for the efficient use of time.

Basic techniques must be taught and repetition of movement is a necessity. One interpretation of skilled behavior is that it is consistently good and unlikely to be disrupted by various distractors. Skilled behavior is also reflected by adaptations and adjustments as they are needed. A skilled person knows how and what to anticipate, and to use the right strategies during competition. It's impossible to teach children to be prepared for every conceivable occurrence in an athletic event, and to make athletes robots is not the answer. They need to be encouraged to think, analyze and problem solve so that they will be best prepared for future unique situations. This learning process takes time and patience on your part, but will help produce better athletes and more fulfilled children.

Reinforcement. We all like to do well. As achievement comes, motivation is elevated, self-confidence becomes stronger, and performance improves. Athletes should be given opportunities and challenges compatible with their capabilities. A challenge too low is boring, while one too great leads to failure, frustration and disinterest.

Reinforcement can be derived from one's own interpretation of a performance or by feedback from someone else, like the coach. In either case, an evaluation of performance in terms of being successful or failing, good or bad, is important in determining the future interest, perseverance and achievement in sport.

Greater efforts should be made to encourage kids to compare their athletic performance with their previous ones rather than with others' performance. This results in self-competition versus the traditional other-competition. Many times, kids play well but lose in a game. Their performance may have improved over the last time, yet they are criticized and dejected for losing when they played well. Why not praise, encourage and look for the good when it exists despite a loss in competition?

Rewards. Our society places tremendous reliance on material rewards. Kids and adults don't want to do anything unless they get "something." The real shame of it all in sport is that kids love to play, take risks, self-evaluate, overcome challenges, and generally, do many of the things usually associated with good sports programs.

Then we introduce the notion of winners and losers, of trophies, ribbons and other recognitions. Soon, children are participating in sport for the sake of rewards rather than for the more ideal values usually associated with athletic experiences.

Rewards should only be used if necessary. They can help create an interest in an activity and shape behavior. But for kids already intrinsically motivated to participate in sports, rewards will do little to help and may do more harm than good. They may change the source of motivation from playing for enjoyment and wanting to develop skills, to looking forward to taking home some prize as an outcome of victory.

Favorable attitudes toward activity can be sustained through a variety of suitable means as alternatives to a reward system. Practice and games that are exciting, personally rewarding, beneficial, and fun will continually stir up the young athlete's interests in sports and encourage him or her to enjoy sporting experiences for many years. Is this not one of the major goals of youth sports programs?

Emotions. The highly skilled athlete has learned to integrate muscular responses correctly and to demonstrate them at the right moment, as well as to use emotions appropriately. Feelings play a great role in how we learn and perform. Being too excitable or anxious will disrupt any coordinated effort; learning and performance are impaired. If emotions are too low, this may indicate a loss of motivation and under-attentiveness, also resulting in poor performance. There is an optimal level of emotions, or arousal, for each kid and activity. Help each kid discover his or her level. (See page 84, Figure 1.)

You should be sensitive to the demands of the activity and the potential reactions of the kids. Some activities can produce fear. Learning to hit a pitched baseball, to dive, to do advanced gymnastic skills, and to ski are examples. Fear blocks learning. Yelling and screaming at kids won't help. Security and confidence have to be gradually built up, and when this occurs, it's amazing how much skills learning can occur.

Every child has different fears and levels of them although certain situations can usually be identified as potentially having a greater or lesser influence on most children. Consequently, analyze each learning situation and each kid carefully. Modify practice techniques if necessary and show the young athletes understanding and sympathy when needed.

Conditioning. Remember that a child must be able to practice correctly and sufficiently if performance is to improve measurably. Strength, endurance, flexibility and speed related specifically to the skills to be learned, must be developed in the athlete. A careful analysis of the demands of the skills will suggest the minimum physical attributes that should be present.

Some of the youngsters may need to be provided with special exercises. Practice of the correct movements requires the presence of adequate physical capabilities. Tips on conditioning are described in Chapter 4.

Underlying movements. As the typical kid reaches eight or so, it is probable that nothing that is to be learned is completely new. Principles of the transfer of learning operate. Newly introduced sports skills require the child to put together once experienced movements in an altered sequence, in a more refined way, possibly with the use of projectiles and special equipment.

A good coaching technique is to show the learners the relationship between learned movements and new ones. The tennis serve and overhand volleyball serve are based on a smooth throwing pattern. If a kid has developed this pattern and understands the relationship between throwing and serving, the serving will be learned more easily and quickly.

Basic movement fundamentals such as throwing, catching, balancing, kicking and running underlie the potential for achievement in a number of sports. A wide range of movement experiences in early childhood should facilitate the acquisition of specific athletic skills.

Analyzing the Young Athlete

In the preceding discussion about emotions, it was suggested that you show considerable attention to each athlete with respect to anxieties. Actually, emotions represent but one of many characteristics associated with athletic achievement. As we can see in Figure 1, an unbelievable assortment of personal attributes should be considered as they vary from kid to kid.

Some are obvious to detect. Many are not. Take a simple matter such as sensory impairment, for instance. Many children have been diagnosed as being slow learners or mentally retarded until it was realized that they suffered from visual or hearing impairments which impeded their performances and led to a misclassification. In the learning of many sports skills, it is also imperative that the sense organs be in good shape. If not, such limitations will work to the disadvantage of the young athlete.

You should maintain a personal record for each athlete, considering as many factors as you can and update it regularly. This information will give you a better idea as to what to expect from the kids with regard to athletic performance and general behavior, and will suggest the instructional and personal approaches you might take.

Keep in mind that

1. All children do not learn at the same rate.

2. All children do not respond to the same instructional approach in the same way.

3. The greater the ideal presence of personal attributes associated with achievements in a particular sport, the greater the potential will be realized.

4. Personal limitations can be compensated for (for example, hustle can overcome certain deficits in size or skill).

5. Children have different motives, values and interests.

6. Children come from different types of families and have various types of influences and pressures.

7. Children have different experiences and dissimilar potential for athletic success.

8. Children mature at different rates, thus producing a dissimilar potential for learning and performance.

Pondering these individual difference considerations (and those in Figure 1) is enough to make a grown person shudder! If you have to consider so many distractions among kids, how do you begin to coach them? How is it possible to reconcile all these factors and somehow help every kid to reach his or her athletic potential in the limited time you have to work with them?

FIGURE 1

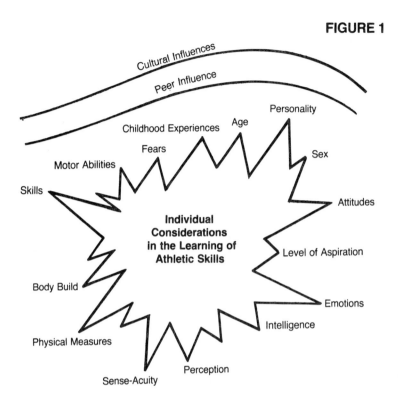

Let's be realistic. You can't. But you can think about them. You can be sensitive to differences in kids and alert to what these may mean in athletic potential and performance. Whenever possible and when time permits, give individual instruction and counsel.

It's much more difficult to design and manage instruction for individuals than groups. But the more heterogeneous the kids in the group are, the more they need special considerations. The more alike they are, the easier it is to treat them similarly. At the very least, try to devise strategies that will accommodate the hopes and capabilities of the young athletes who expect guidance — and understanding.

Some Specific Coaching Tips Concerning Learning Processes

We now turn to some procedural techniques that might generally be applicable to most young learners. Of course, we have already suggested a number of them. Look back at the advice provided in "Getting the Idea" and "General Practice Considerations." Also, after reading "The Child's Capabilities" and "Analyzing Athletic Activities," you should be able to draw out implications for instruction. Here are some more tips.

1. Memory. We do many things at the moment and then seemingly forget them. How many times have you looked up a phone number in a phone book, dialed it, got a busy signal, went to dial it again, and were embarrassed because you had to look up the number again — even though you had just dialed it 10 seconds previously? Sure. It happens to all of us.

Learning motor skills requires certain principles that can be followed to promote the way they are retained over time. Mental rehearsal is one technique: thinking through the act, thinking about it, helps to improve its retention. Have kids think about what they are to do, and after they have done it, rehearse it mentally.

2. Relaxed Concentration. During the act itself, it does no good to think too much of the details of the movement. The skilled athlete gets the right image of the act and executes it, focusing on the minimal number of relevant cues.

Help the kids to identify the single most important cue or cues at the moment and to focus on them. As skill levels change, so might the cues. Skilled performance is smooth, correctly sequenced and timed, when there is minimal conscious intervention during the activity. Promote concentration as much as possible, as distractions cause variable performances.

3. Anticipation. The importance of anticipation cannot be emphasized enough. As a person becomes skilled, less attention to the immediate activity is required, so that more can be directed toward subsequent possibilities. The mental system can be freed to anticipate, but it is another matter as to whether in fact the athlete does anticipate.

We might even suggest that in externally paced activities, proficiency is reflected in part by the anticipatory powers of the athlete. Expecting what might happen, being prepared to react accordingly, and then doing the right things is what skill is all about. You should prepare athletes to think ahead. Cue them. Guide them. Soon they will do it on their own.

4. General Athletic Ability. Don't expect that a kid who is good in one sport will necessarily be as effective in another sport. There are many abilities, no one general athletic or general motor ability. To the extent that sports are similar in the demands placed on the athletes, we might expect similar levels of performance. But that's all.

With very young children, there is a greater tendency to see the same kids excelling in various sports. That's because size, maturity and strength underlie achievement to a great extent. With development, skills become more sophisticated. Each sport requires a greater amount of specific practice for athletes to excel in relation to others, and athletes become differentiated. Some will practice very diligently at a variety of activities. They may be very motivated to achieve well in a number of endeavors. They may even fulfill this desire. But by and large, it is more realistic to expect accomplishments in sports to be individualistic with increasing age, with the so-called all-round athlete more an exception than a rule.

5. Providing Information. Instructions and observation of others help the young athlete get an idea of what is to be learned. But what happens after an attempt is made to accomplish the objective? Ideally, the kid will feel or see how he did and attempt to modify behaviors accordingly. But the beginner does not usually do this well. Here is where you come in, to provide information to the athlete about his or her performance. A young athlete will not improve without knowledge about performance and its results.

Initially, the child depends on extra help for guidance which should be provided as soon as possible in connection with performance, and as specific as he or she can handle. Yet the child should learn how to interpret his or her performance; this comes with experience and the direction provided by the coach. The less "natural" feedback there is available to the performer, in such sports as diving, swimming, gymnastics, the more the dependence on the coach for information. The ultimate goal is to help make the athlete more self-reliant and self-dependent.

Telling the kid how he or she did provides guidance for subsequent actions. It also shows an interest in the athlete and can be a source of motivation. There may be a number of activities in which children can be paired off, with one practicing the skill to be learned and the other providing feedback. This procedure obviously works out better with older athletes. In large groups where it is almost impossible for one coach to recognize the efforts of many athletes, pairing off the kids for mutual assistance can be helpful.

Coaching Tips On Practice Strategies

When organizing and arranging practice sessions, a number of questions can be raised as to how to best teach skills for most children. Invariably, trade-offs can be anticipated in decision-making: you may gain one thing and lose something else. Then again, in some cases, there may be clear-cut advantages to one possible coaching method versus another one. Let's identify some possible alternative practice strategies.

1. Highly Guided Learning vs. Problem Solving Learning. Obviously you can attempt to structure the learning experience so that kids are conditioned to respond as you cue them. Or, you can have them try to acquire skills spontaneously in a trial and error manner.

Guided learning is highly efficient, leading to specifically acquired behaviors. Problem-solving learning takes more time but increases the probability of adapting to new but related situations. Of course, your practice sessions could and possibly should reflect both kinds of learning. A careful analysis of both the activities you are teaching and the current and potential future demands on the athletes will help you decide how much emphasis should be placed on guided *(product)* learning versus problem solving *(process)* learning.

2. Part vs. Whole Teaching Methods. Many activities can be broken down into parts for purposes of instruction, or taught in their entirety. Take the crawl stroke in swimming for example. One could teach the leg kick, arm stroke, and breathing separately or together. The golf swing could be separated into parts and taught that way, or taught as a "whole."

As a general rule,
    simple activities: whole method
    difficult activities: part method $\longrightarrow$ whole method

In other words, if an activity requires movements that are synchronized sequentially and/or at any one time, it probably can be learned under the whole method of instruction. The crawl stroke requires different body movements to occur at the same time, and probably should be learned with a part method of instruction.

3. Massed vs. Distributed Practice. There is only so much time to practice and so many skills we hope children will learn well. Should practice be continuous (massed) on one activity? Should practice in that activity be separated frequently with rest periods or with practice in other activities (distributed)?

Continuous practice is undesirable with younger children because their attention span is relatively brief and tends to wander. Changes in practice regimens and activities should liven things up and diminish loss of attention and motivation. As children get older and/or skill increases, massed practice is accepted more readily and can be as effective as distributed practice in the long run.

4. Sequence of Activities. As a guiding principle, activities should be taught in such a manner that

a. they are arranged hierarchically in a sequence in order for the the mastery of one level of activities to enable the learner to master the next level of activities, and so on.

b. they promote positive transfer effects, namely, the learning of one activity will facilitate the learning of the next activity.

An analysis of the final skill hoped for in an activity and the level of skill at which the kids are located at any given time should lead to the identification and logical sequencing of activities. An example of sequential analysis of an activity appears in Figure 2.

5. Simulators vs. "Real" Experience. One of the ultimate objectives of your program is to prepare kids for competition. Practice conditions should closely resemble contest situations as soon as and as much as possible, and allow kids to practice under modified conditions if the skills are extremely complex or progress is poor.

There are many pieces of equipment on the market for virtually every sport, designed to assist learners in certain activities. Ball throwing machines in tennis and baseball, swimming aids, football devices, etc., are geared to simplify learning experiences. They can be quite beneficial, but athletes may tend to rely on them too much if used too often. Once objectives are reached, learning devices should be discarded if learning to perform under real conditions is to be realized.

Many times, however, real experiences are unavailable. For example, when cold weather and snow preclude outdoor practice, modified indoor practice can help athletes maintain the skills they have acquired.

6. Practice and Contest Conditions. To restate an important principle, *practice conditions should simulate contest conditions*

Beginner's Ice Hockey Program — A Partial Learning Hierarchy

The learner should make demonstrable improvement in his mastery of the fundamental skills of ice hockey and develop an enthusiasm to practice diligently both at the hockey clinic and on his own. He should also be eager to participate in ice hockey clinics and formal practice sessions.

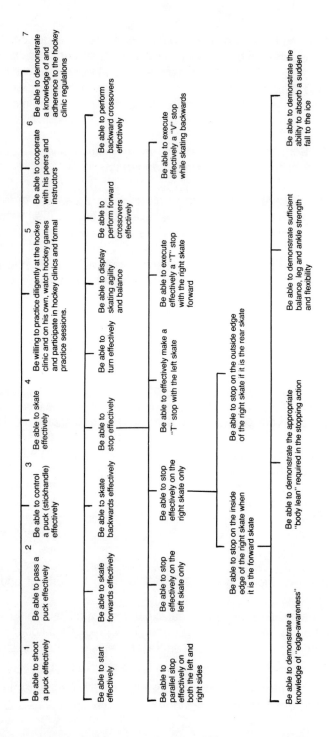

as soon as possible. Kids will have to perform in front of spectators. They will perform under the emotional pressures of competition, of winning and losing, perhaps under conditions of fatigue and even minor injury.

As athletes become more acquainted with competitive contest situations, they will learn to perform more effectively. With more experience for the kids in actual athletic contests and practices closely resembling them, we should expect familiarization to breed desirable athletic behavior. As basic skills are learned, why not think of ways to make practice sessions more "real" to better prepare athletes for what will be expected of them?

7. Speed vs. Accuracy. As you may realize, there is optimal quickness and accuracy in movement that we try to teach kids to attain in many skills. Assuming that both factors may be equally important in skilled performance, should you initially teach the act slowed down, with emphasis on the movement and form? Should you emphasize speed, reasoning that accuracy will come later? Or should you emphasize speed and precision equally in your instruction?

The usual approach is to stress movement, form and accuracy, gradually increasing the speed of execution as practice proceeds. Yet, it might be detrimental to do this. A child could learn a tennis stroke very well and hit the ball very gently. But under competitive conditions, he or she eventually will have to hit firmer and harder. The movement must be quickened.

Although it may be more frustrating at first to practice a skill under both speed and accuracy conditions, this may be the best approach in the long run. With speed we lose accuracy and with accuracy we lose speed. In the tennis example, although accuracy in stroking was gained initially, it was, in a sense, attained under "false" conditions. Later the stroke must be modified to produce a harder hit. If the youngster started out stroking firmly, the best effects would have been realized. Once again you are reminded of the general rule that practice conditions should resemble contest conditions as much as possible.

There are exceptions to this rule, of course. A child who has difficulty in improving may need extra attention and special practice conditions. It would be better to slow the movement down so that certain problems can be worked out. You certainly want to minimize frustration and lack of achievement.

Putting It All Together Systematically

1. Analyze carefully the skills and activities that are to be taught, considering the ideal sequence to achieve your objectives.
2. Analyze sensitively the children under your direction to become aware of the general behavioral and skill characteristics of the group, as well as individual differences.
3. Attempt to apply information you have read here to the way you design instruction for your practice sessions, for coaching is both an art and a science.

A systematic analysis suggests a more scientific approach to the analysis of your athletes, your situation and the skills to be taught. These considerations should enable you to deal more effectively with children as you attempt to teach them skills and to coach them in athletic contests.

Learning is a complex process but one of your major roles is to help children learn skills, knowledges and favorable attitudes related to the sport. Start with the philosophy that every child deserves to learn and to improve. You can promote this process if you are knowledgeable about the sport, children, and how to communicate with them.

Shaping Up for Competition

Chapter 4

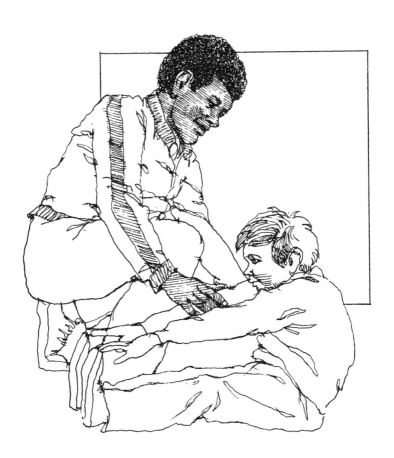

Ronald Byrd
University of Alabama in Birmingham

Training, conditioning or getting into shape all mean simply increasing physical fitness. Most of you have your own ideas as to what makes a person physically fit, but there are some important concepts related specifically to youth sports.

FITNESS FUNDAMENTALS

First, what are the components of physical fitness and how should they be ranked in importance? Most coaches agree that flexibility, strength and endurance are basic. Speed is a factor which, combined with strength, is termed power. Endurance can be subdivided into local muscular endurance and cardiovascular endurance. Balance, coordination and other factors might also be listed. You rank these in importance by the sport. Flexibility in the shoulders would be very important to a swimmer, while to a second basemen, coordination might be of more concern. Power is critical in football, and soccer players must have good cardiovascular endurance.

The emphasis on conditioning also depends on the level of competition. The younger the athlete, the more stress you should put on technique and skill, even at the expense of conditioning. Getting in shape is simply not as important for youngsters learning the basics. A minimal level is necessary to prevent injuries, but only when competition and winning become more significant does conditioning become more a matter of concern. This is true for two reasons. First, with the development of speed and power that naturally accompanies maturation, young athletes are more likely to subject their bodies to levels of stress that cause injuries. Compare the forces in tackling by 8 and 14-year-old boys, or the centrifugal forces and likelihood of turning an ankle in rounding first base at full speed by children of widely different ages. Second, conditioning is less important for younger athletes because there are fewer opportunities to take part in sports or events in which conditioning could be decisive. The length of games is less, fields are smaller, and races shorter.

You should plan training with specific outcomes in mind, such as stretching for flexibility, doing high intensity work for strength, and exercising over long periods of time to develop endurance. Because practice time with young athletes is limited, you should gear training to the demands of the specific sport. Jogging and pushups contribute to overall health and fitness, although they are generally wasteful in terms of conditioning for participation in sports. For athletes in training, runners should run, swimmers should swim, and coaches in other sports should select conditioning activities as closely related to the sport as possible. For example, rather than have baseball players jog laps, they should do repeated short sprints with sharp, full-speed turns, preferably on a baseball diamond. Pitchers develop the specific endurance they need by throwing. One of the best exercises for soccer players is repeated kicking. Exploding off the line for short distances is valuable in developing power for football players. Set up your team's basic conditioning program based on a careful analysis of the physical requirements of your specific sport. Advanced fitness for advanced athletes requires more time and so the inclusion of some general conditioning can be better justified.

Why are the results of training so specific? The body is extremely efficient, adapting exactly to the demands placed on it. If you ask it to adjust to watching television or sitting at a desk, it responds by changing to the levels of strength and endurance required. Conversely, if you *overload* a body by unaccustomed physical stresses, physiological adaptations occur which make the stress more manageable. For example, the first time a young trackster runs a seven-minute mile in training, the overload might make it difficult to complete. But when repeating this seven-minute mile every day, the body gradually adapts to the point where the run is no longer as strenuous. With adaptation, a plateau in performance is achieved because the stress is no longer an overload. Progression then becomes the key to higher levels of fitness and a new level of stress must be established. This can be done by training at a faster pace or over longer distances, depending on whether increases in speed or in endurance are more important. These basic concepts of specificity, overload and progression apply to the development of any aspect of fitness at any level of athletic competition.

Athletes may differ greatly in their physical response to conditioning. Some seem to increase in fitness by leaps and bounds; others get little or no benefit. Any very rapid change in strength, endurance or other form of fitness probably results from psychological adjustments to the task; physiological adaptation requires a longer time. Rate of maturation should also be considered. Early maturers may perform quite well in youth sport, but be subsequently outstripped by late maturing athletes. Maturation does not only mean body size. In fact, maturity in terms of specific functions such as coordination, speed, etc., might be more important for coaches of young athletes to consider. If a youngster isn't endowed with physical abilities, no amount of coaching will make him or her an outstanding athlete. It might seem unfair, but the genetically superior child will probably excel regardless of coaching or conditioning programs. In either case, your job as coach is critical in encouraging young athletes toward reaching their potential.

NUTRITION

Nutrition is critical to young athletes. A balanced diet with foods from the four basic groups is essential. As a coach, you have little direct influence in this respect; however, if a player is often fatigued, you might discover poor dietary habits are to blame, and tactful suggestions to the player and parents might be helpful. You can also sometimes help the obviously malnourished or overweight boy or girl by such counseling. However, most nutritional problems are not usually obvious during relatively short sport seasons. You should spend some team time emphasizing the fundamentals of nutrition and how proper nutrition affects performance. Such information is usually presented in classrooms, but it generally assumes special meaning coming from a coach.

All through childhood, but especially just before and during the adolescent growth spurt, there are unique nutritional needs. While the need for protein in college-age and older athletes has often been grossly overestimated, the growing young athlete needs greater quantities. It is imperative that essential amino acids (protein components) be present in the diet, ideally in eggs, meats and dairy products. For vegetarians, a variety of fruits and vegetables must be eaten to ensure adequate quantities of the essential amino acids.

Milk and other dairy products meet the great need for calcium and phosphorous for bone growth. Iron and vitamin deficiencies caused by an inadequate supply of fruits, vegetables, and enriched cereals and bread are not unusual, particularly in children of low-income families. The most common bad food habits are: (1) poor or no breakfast, (2) inadequate lunches, (3) too much snacking, and (4) irregular eating habits. Ironically, participating in youth sports doesn't always help to alleviate these practices because of conflicts with mealtime and the ready availability of snacks.

Another common nutritional problem is childhood obesity. This is very serious for two reasons. The obese children are penalized in athletics because they tire more quickly. The increased inertia makes quick starts, stops and changes of direction in running much more difficult for them. Second, and more important, obesity imposes a heavy penalty of poor health throughout life. Overweight people are more susceptible to many maladies, the most important being cardiovascular disease. The younger the person, the better the chance of overcoming obesity and the greater the prospect for healthier adult life. What do you, the coach, have to do with this? The coach is a respected and influential person to kids. Coaching that includes attention to values and to health as well as to the sport itself, can have a powerful effect on the lives of players.

"Making weight," the process of losing weight to participate in a weight classification, is common in sports such as football, judo and wrestling. This practice, which is done by dieting, sweating heavily to lose water weight, or by inducing vomiting or diarrhea, is firmly opposed by The American Medical Association. The advantage gained by playing against naturally smaller children is more than offset by the potential harm of such an unhealthy approach. A coach could be legally liable for recommending or encouraging making weight if an athlete suffers any serious result.

The young athlete who wants or "needs" to gain weight is a less critical problem. "Needing" to gain weight for sports is questionable. The best, most efficient athletes are lean. Smallness is certainly a disadvantage in many competitive situations, but the size of the athlete might be entirely normal for his or her present level of maturity. Retarded growth may occur from malnutrition, but usually maturation and normal growth take care of what is probably only a temporary inconvenience rather than a serious problem. Don't automatically recommend an increase in food intake; there is seldom a good reason for simply padding the body with fatty tissue. First, look at the parents for genetic influence. Are they also small or lean? If not, find out if there is a possibility of poor dietary habits.

With regard to pre-game meals, allow about two hours between eating and playing to permit time for digestion to be completed if the meal is primarily carbohydrate, as it should be. Proteins and fats are slower to digest and may remain in the stomach for hours, hindering performance in some athletes. This is less of a potential problem in young athletes than for those subjected to more intense, longer competitive situations. Unless you are coaching age-group swimmers or runners involved in long distance events, pre-game eating patterns don't demand much attention.

ENVIRONMENT

The young athlete can adapt to environmental stresses as well as to the physical stresses of conditioning. The body adjusts to heat, cold or altitude in very specific ways that make subsequent exposures less stressful. The most common problem of environmental stress occur either during play in a relatively different environment, or during pre-season or early season practices when boys or girls are still unacclimatized. There are sound arguments for and against post-season regional, national and international playoffs or championships. Since the situations exist for some sports, you must consider the physiological effects of playing in special environments.

You should also accept the fact that players coming out for practice may not be well adapted to the climate for two reasons: (1) practice may begin at the onset of seasonal changes when there has been neither sufficient time nor exposure to the hotter or colder weather for adjustments to occur, and (2) many children tend to avoid the discomfort of extremes of heat or cold, which limits their acclimatization.

Cold

Temperature alone is not a complete index of the degree of stress. Dry cold is less chilling than wet cold, and wind adds to the stress in either case. Examples of the effect of wind are presented below. It is important for you to realize that whether the wind is blowing at 10 mph or the athlete is running in calm air at 10 mph, the chilling effect is the same.

Equivalent temperatures in windy conditions

Thermometer readings (°F)

Wind	40	30	20	10
None	40	30	20	10
10mph	28	17	4	-9
20mph	18	4	-10	-25
30mph	13	-2	-18	-33

Your primary concern in cold exposure should be prevention of injuries. The younger the athlete, the less the chance of muscle pulls from inadequate warm-up. But because of the great differences between individuals' susceptibility to such injuries, you should never allow play or practice without adequate warm-up. The amount necessary is influenced by proper clothing. Warm-up suits and uniforms should be light, loose and in layers for best insulation. Vinyl, nylon or other such waterproof warm-up clothing should be removed when the athlete starts to sweat, to allow evaporation. If there are periodic breaks in the action, replacement of clothing may be necessary to prevent heat loss. Obviously, coaches and bench jockeys producing less heat than active athletes have to wear enough clothing to prevent excessive heat loss.

Excessive cold exposure, generally of exposed skin, causes chilblains and frostbite. The red, itching skin of chilblains is not dangerous but is a warning that the exposure is at least bordering on excessive. Frostbite is another matter; the damage to tissues caused by this critical injury requires immediate medical attention. Frostbite can range from freezing with itching and numbness to tissue death.

Loss of manual dexterity in the cold can result in injuries to the hands and fingers. Other injuries may result because of the loss of "feel" and grip strength in the hands. An example could be in losing control of a bat or hockey stick and thus hurting another player.

Physical fitness level is directly related to the extent of regular physical activity. Unfortunately, during the winter many youngsters are less active than at other times of the year. Thus, if injuries are prevented by proper use of clothing and warmup, winter sports can be most valuable, making an important contribution to health and fitness.

Heat

The challenge in exercising in hot weather is to dissipate rather than conserve heat as is the task in a cold environment. Evaporation of sweat is the primary means of ridding the body of the excess heat produced by muscular activity. Clothing interferes with evaporation, so young athletes should wear loose, light-colored, porous uniforms. The less clothing the better in a hot environment. Although protective padding is necessary in some sports, it is an insulator and can cause heat-related complications. Obese children have built-in insulation in their fat and are more sensitive to heat stress.

High humidity aggravates heat exposure because it hinders the evaporation of sweat. Wind and cloudiness also affect the severity of any degree of heat stress. The difficulty in simultaneously considering heat, humidity, air movement, and cloud cover is obvious. The most practical approach is probably subjectively to judge the environmental conditions and watch for excessive stress in the players.

Overexposure to heat can range in severity from muscular cramping to heat exhaustion and heat stroke. Heat cramps can be prevented by adding salt to the diet. There is little if any reason to subject children to heat stress levels which call for salt tablets. Salting their food should always be adequate. Salt depletion can also lead to heat exhaustion, as can excessive water loss. Heat exhaustion is characterized by dizziness, fainting, loss of physical and/or mental coordination, and a cold skin. Rest, replacement of water and salt, and medical consultation should follow. *Heat stroke* is an extremely serious disorder requiring *immediate* medical attention. Symptoms are a hot, dry skin, temperature 105° F, and irrational behavior.

Any sign of a player's inability to cope with the combined stresses of heat and exercise should be taken seriously. Because children are relatively less able to handle heat stress, coaches have a great responsibility and should be conservative in any situation where doubts exist concerning how to proceed. Unfortunately, there continue to be heat-related deaths in athletics, most of them attributable to illogical practices by coaches.

What else can you do to prevent such a tragedy? Constant and close observation of individuals under stress is basic. Second, and probably most important, every player should have access to water at any time and be encouraged to drink before, during, and after activity. Commercial glucose-electrolyte solutions may be used, but plain water is adequate. Third, practices and games should, if possible, be scheduled in the early morning or in the evening after sunset if environmental conditions so dictate. Finally, acclimatization to heat stress should take place over a period of one to two weeks by actually exercising in the heat at gradually increasing intensities and for longer periods of time each day. Children should not be rushed into competition or heavy conditioning without such insurance.

Altitude

Exposure to altitudes over 5,000 feet reduces the athlete's ability to supply oxygen to the working muscles. This is detrimental in sports requiring much cardiovasclar stress, but is unimportant in activities requiring less sustained exercise. Distance running, distance swimming, and soccer would be affected while baseball and football would not. Best performance is within 24 hours of arrival, unless weeks of exposure is possible. Any sightseeing in connection with competition at a high altitude should follow, rather than precede a game. There is less real danger for the young athlete from this stress than from cold or heat exposure.

Inclement Weather

The decision as to whether or not to play or practice in inclement weather should rest solely on the welfare of the child. If you feel there is increased danger of injury, you must cancel. Practicing in the rain may be dangerous in baseball or soccer, but benefit runners who would profit from better heat dissipation by a cooling shower. Unless there is lightning, in which case play should cease, no blanket recommendation concerning inclement weather can be made. Rain and snow pose no particular physiologic threat beyond the possibility of playing surfaces, balls and other equipment becoming so slippery that injuries might result. The loss of important practice time, or a game having to be rescheduled should never influence your decision. The only thing the matters is, "Is the health or safety of a child likely to suffer?"

SPECIAL CONDITIONS

Physical Examinations

Physical examinations are routinely required of high school and college athletes. They are too often not compulsory for the young athlete. There is no logical basis for this inconsistency. Children in organized sports programs should have an annual physical. It is unrealistic to expect to have a team physician, but you may ask parents to take the child to the family physician. Volunteer or low-cost screening is also often available from interested physicians or through a local health department or medical society. Whether the decision is an unqualified OK to play, a conditional OK, disqualification, or a suspension following treatment and/or re-examination, you must respect the decision of the physician. (For a medical opinion regarding physical examinations, see page 95.)

Injuries

Because of the lack of an on-the-field physician, a heavy bruden is placed on you as a coach. You are responsible for giving first-aid. You must judge the severity of injuries, and you must decide whether a boy or girl should continue to play. Under the pressure of competition, you must make quick decisions that will not only affect the outcome of the contest, but can also have long lasting effects on the player's health.

Generally, if an injury is serious enough to necessitate the removal of a player from game, you should not gamble by returning the boy or girl to competition without referral to a physician and a written release by a physician. Less severe injuries require your on-the-field judgment of each case.

Never take any player's complaints lightly. Some injuries are obvious; in some instances your patience and judgment will be tested. Rarely, cases of sudden death in young athletes occur. Almost inevitably, there was a history of ignored symptoms of cardiovascular disease. Unfortunately, we associate rapid pulse, paleness, nausea, labored breathing, and chest pain with heart disease only in adults. The fact is that congenital defects may escape a physician's notice during a physical examination, but show up during the stress of practice or play. All such cases should be referred to a physician for careful evaluation. While such defects are rare, the death of a child that you are coaching would be more tragic if you could have prevented it.

While most injuries are not severe, you must always be mindful of the safety of your players. The following are not meant to be all-inclusive. Every sport and every situation present their own hazards. However, the overall incidence of injuries can be reduced by:

1. Proper and thorough warmups
2. Good conditioning, both pre-season and in-season
3. Use of good quality and well-fitting equipment
4. Good maintenance of playing areas
5. Well planned, relatively short practices
6. Use of capable officials
7. Pre-season physical examinations
8. Knowledge of first aid by the coach
9. Readiness of the coach to refer the injured to a physician
10. Unwillingness to expose any child to undue risk of injury or of aggravation of an existing injury.

Drugs

The use of drugs to improve athletic performance is generally discouraged and is cause for disqualification by most sport associations. Unfortunately, both prescription and non-prescription drugs are too often available and used, even in youth sports. While small advantages in performance or trainability can sometimes be gained, there are potentially harmful side effects that can result from disturbing one's normal physiology. Apart from the side effects, some drugs are habit forming and others remove built-in safety factors. Worst of all might be the development of permissiveness or even positive attitudes towards drugs in general. There are sound biological, ethical, and legal reasons for not being a part of the athletic drug scene. There is no substitute for proper conditioning and good coaching.

SUMMARY

Shaping up for competition is a complex process requiring attention to all sorts of details. Penalties for inadequate training include poor performance and a high incidence of injuries. But when your team is well-conditioned, among your rewards is the knowledge that you have contributed toward enabling each boy or girl to experience the highest level of success consistent with innate ability.

Getting Them Up, Not Uptight

Chapter 5

Linda Bunker and Robert Rotella
University of Virginia

The Right Coach is Crucial

The head coach of a competitive youth sports team is in a very enjoyable, yet challenging and responsible position because the years between age 8 to 18 are crucial to each child's physical and psychological development. The participants in youth sports are searching for understanding of both themselves and those surrounding them. The youth coach must know how to help each athlete on the team develop his or her potential to the fullest. Athletes who are taught to feel good about their potential will enjoy practicing and seek additional instruction. We must turn *all* athletes on to sport rather than turn some on and some off, depending on how high or low we perceive their ability.

The coach can have as close a relationship with the young athlete as almost any other person besides the child's parents. The coach's behavior and attitude are often a model for the players. If the coach is positive and confident, the athletes are likely to assume these characteristics.

To help each member of the team perform to the best of his or her ability the coach must realize the importance of the athlete's mental attitude and emotional control, two variables that often separate great athletes from mediocre athletes and successful teams from mediocre teams.

It is vital that coaches of young athletes bear two points in mind. First, the young athlete is in the most important, formative years and must learn how to handle the anxieties associated with sport performance. Second, some youngsters who may not appear to have physical or psychological characteristics likely to lead them to a high level of athletic success are far too often eliminated from sport participation before they are 12 years old. This practice is unacceptable. With care and guidance, many of these young participants can have many positive experiences and develop into fine athletes as they mature.

Following is a "Letter to My Football Coach" describing a negative coach relationship:

Dear Coach:
You won't remember me. It was just a few years back. I was one of those kids that turn out every year for freshman football without the slightest idea of how to play the game. Think hard. I was the tall, skinny kid, a little slower than the others.

Still don't remember? Well, I remember you. I remember how scared I was of you when you'd slap your hands together and yell "Hit!" I remember how you used to laugh at me and guys like me when we'd miss a tackle or get beat one on one in practice.

You see, you never let me play in a game. Once in a while, when you'd be giving a chalk talk to the first string, I'd get to play a couple of downs of scrimmage.

I really admired you. We all did. But now that I'm a little older and a little wiser, I just wanted to let you know that you blew it. I didn't play football after my freshman year. You convinced me that I didn't have what it took, that I wasn't tough enough.

I remember the first day of practice, when you asked for all the linebackers. I wanted to be a linebacker. The first time I tried to tackle someone I got my helmet ripped off. All I had done was lower my head and hit. No technique. No tackle.

You laughed. You told me I ought to be a quarterback, that I tackled like one. All the guys laughed. You were really funny.

Another time, after I became a guard, I missed a block — in practice. Of course. The guy sidestepped and I wound up with a face mask in the mud.

"C'mon! You hit like a girl," you said. I wanted to hit. I wanted to tell you how much I wanted to hit. But if I had, you'd have flattened me because you were tough and didn't take any back talk.

We ran the play again, and I hit the same guy a pretty good shot this time. When I looked at you, you were talking to another coach.

I'm the first to admit that I was pretty bad. Even if I had been coached on technique, I still would have been a lousy football player. I was one of those kids who was a couple of years behind my peers in physical maturity and strength.

That's where you messed up. I grew up. By the time I was a senior, I stood 6'5" and weighed 220. I couldn't fly, but I could run pretty well. That non-athletic freshman could now throw a baseball harder than anyone in the state. I was drafted and signed by a major league baseball team.

When my strength started to increase about my junior year, the varsity coaches drove me crazy with requests to turn out for football. I told them I didn't like the game.

"But why not? You're a natural!"

"I dunno, Coach, I can't explain it. Football is just not my game."

Looking back I really regret not playing football. It would have been a lot of fun. Maybe I could even have helped the team. But thanks to you, I turned against the game before I ever really got into it. A little coaching, a little encouragement, and who knows? I guess I'll never find out.

You're still out there, I see, coaching the frosh and sounding mean. I wonder how many potentially good athletes, kids that are a year or two behind, that you will discourage this year? How many of them will be the butt of your jokes?

It took me a while to learn that your "toughness" is meaningless. You're just a guy who played a little second string in college. So what have you got to be so tough about?

How sad. You're in a position to do a lot of boys a lot of good. But I doubt that you will. You'll never give up a chance to look "tough" and sound "tough." You think that's what football's all about.

I know better.

Larry D. Brooks

From *Scholastic Coach,* January 1976,
New York, New York.

Some youngsters may never become great athletes, but they, too, need and deserve just as much time and attention from the coach. The goal should be to foster an enjoyable and motivationally attractive environment so that these youngsters remain involved in sports at the appropriate level of competition.

There are many ways to encourage a positive mental attitude in practices and games. Participants in youth sports are usually highly motivated to listen to the coach, learn and improve their skills. The coach must be sure to maintain and increase this highly motivated state.

Emphasize the Positive

We must emphasize the positive, rather than the negative, aspects of each individual's performance. Situations should be planned, especially in the early stages of practice, to make the young athlete feel successful. If the young athlete leaves practice with feelings of pride rather than shame, he/she will continue to be attracted to sports, be interested in discovering weaknesses or mistakes and be willing to correct them.

Young athletes have had a limited range of experiences. They don't know if they have great, average or poor athletic ability. Youngsters who are constantly told that they are talented and are made to feel that way, start believing they are talented and often perform as if they are — a self-fulfilling prophecy. What athletes believe about themselves is often more important than their actual ability.

Initially, young athletes should be frequently and consistently reinforced with verbal praise and general approval for their efforts. Too much criticism will cause children to lose confidence in their ability and therefore lower their aspirations. It takes a special kind of coach to be able to find something good to say to each player. Anyone can hurt a child's ego with, "You blockhead, can't you catch anything but a cold," or "Oh, brother, we've got a butterfingers Bobbie on our team." Such comments can devastate a young athlete's self-concept and desire to participate.

We must find ways to make all children feel good about themselves, even it if is only how well they look in their uniform or how well they run the bases, or block. In time, positive reinforcement and rewards should be handed out with greater selectivity and less frequently. Praise should be given only when the young athlete has improved and deserves it. This approach will increase the athlete's motivation to achieve and make the coach's rewards more meaningful. The result should be an increase in effort and enthusiasm displayed in practice and games.

PEANUTS ®
By cartoonist-of-the-year Charles M. Schulz

Many college and professional coaches use criticism, sarcasm, threats and punishment to motivate a team. The youth coach must recognize that there are important differences between the way top level athletes can be motivated and the techniques most effective for young athletes. Threats and punishment can have a very detrimental effect on the young athlete. Few athletes at that age have the confidence necessary for these techniques to be effective motivators.

If situations arise in which threats or punishments must be used, be certain they are appropriate and follow through with them. Threats of punishments may be somewhat useful if the athletes are winning consistently and are becoming overconfident and less coachable. This approach should certainly be the exception rather than the rule.

It is extremely important to create positive team morale. Cooperative teammates can help each other in learning new skills as well as providing a desirable social environment. The coach can affect the situation significantly by the use of equal time rules to keep all of the athletes happy and motivated and to encourage the more skilled athletes to help their teammates improve their skills. The coach must be sure that athletes of lesser skill are not ridiculed for their mistakes by the more talented players. Emphasis should be on encouraging and rewarding effort.

Awards and Motivation

Youth sport teams typically provide a wide variety of awards — trophies, plaques, jackets, ribbons, certificates — to inspire players to practice and play harder. We must carefully consider the possible positive and negative effects of these rewards in terms of immediate and future performances. Most children enter into youth sports with a high level of intrinsic motivation. They participate because they enjoy it, want to master and control their skills, or feel and look competent, are likely to practice dilligently over long periods and perform at a higher level. They are internally controlled and self-motivated, compared to athletes who participate mainly for a reward. This motivation might be reduced by the frequent distribution of awards so commonplace in today's youth sport programs. Most likely, we are unintentionally causing many youths who were originally intrinsically motivated and attracted to sport to become extrinsically motivated.

The extrinsically motivated child would likely respond with an increase in immediate performance when awards are presented. Extrinsic rewards for children under seven years appear to be quite effective because they are regarded as a bonus. But after the age of seven, children begin to view rewards just for taking part as a bribe, which causes a reduction in motivation. The long-range effects of extrinsic motivation are not nearly as appealing as those of intrinsic motivation. The extrinsically motivated child would likely drop out if rewards were eliminated. Hopefully, youth sport coaches recognize that lifelong performance and enjoyment are more fulfilling than temporary goals.

Awards for Outstanding Performance. Another common practice in youth sports programs is to reward athletes for the quality of their performance, which usually increases their intrinsic motivation. Unfortunately, many young athletes never benefit from these rewards; they don't think they have the ability ever to attain the awards. If we want to help each athlete reach his or her maximal potential, we should make it possible for each child to receive an award. At the beginning of the season, the coach, together with each young athlete, should set specific goals which the athlete must attain to earn the desired award. Care should be taken to insure that each child practices diligently to achieve the award, and that the goals should not be beyond the athlete's ability.

In general, children eight years and older should not be presented with awards merely for participating. Awards related to individually established goals for quality of performance tend to increase intrinsic motivation as long as the child believes he or she is physically able to attain the award.

Anxiety and Performance

Competitive stress can originate from many sources — the nature of the game, from within the individual, coach, teammates, friends, parents, fans — and in a variety of situations (practice before, during and after the game). For most athletes, a sport contest is not relaxing and/or always enjoyable. Often, their behavior is quite different from the way they normally behave off the sports field. It is the emotional involvement which makes sports so attractive and at the same time so frustrating and upsetting to so many youngsters.

By their very nature, sports are likely to produce anxiety. Whenever a young athlete is faced with a competitive situation, doubts about the outcome are apt to surface, causing anxiety. This uncertainty about the outcome causes many of us to spend the days and nights prior to a contest worrying about whether our skills are sufficient to allow us to win. Another source of anxiety is strategy. All teams plan and practice strategies geared to winning, and concern over their effectiveness produces a great deal of anxiety.

Another element likely to cause anxiety is luck. The outcome of any sport contest may be influenced in varying degrees by good or bad "breaks" — a good or bad bounce, an unfortunate injury, a mistaken call by the umpire or referee, a gust of wind, or the sun getting in the athlete's eyes. Luck is always unpredictable. If we think about it rationally, we would realize that good and bad breaks will, by the law of averages, eventually even out. Unfortunately, most of us dwell on the bad breaks rather than the good ones. Bad luck accounts for many losses, but wins are usually because we worked harder! By blaming luck for our defeats we allow emotions to control us, which can be detrimental to athletic performance and to effective coaching decisions.

Anxiety obviously plays an important role in youth sport. Each element in sport can be anxiety arousing. There are, however, many other causes of anxiety in sport which may originate from sources external to the athlete himself or the very nature of sport. The fact that sport holds a revered position in today's world may cause children to establish unrealistic expectations. For example, older athletes are paid enormous salaries, given scholarships to school, and are held in high esteem by a large segment of the population. We reward success in athletics, but we also punish and create feelings of shame among individuals who are unsuccessful in athletics. This system of rewards and punishment attracts children to sport, but it also produces a fear of failure — a major producer of anxiety.

Emphasis on competition and winning can cause young athletes a great deal of stress. As youngsters start to improve, they often raise their level of aspiration to unrealistic heights and are therefore never pleased with themselves. If the young athlete also starts believing that others expect great performances of him/her, the athlete may put himself or herself under even more pressure. This kind of pressure, whether it derives from the participant, parents, friends or the coach, will never allow the athlete to be completely happy with his/her performance.

The youth coach must understand the relationship between anxiety and sport performance and how to maximize healthy emotional development in all young athletes. Anyone who has been alone in an unfamiliar and dark environment knows that fear and anxiety can distort perceptual abilities. Because perceptual abilities are needed for effective sport performance, the overly anxious athlete will not usually react in the appropriate manner.

Anxiety can also distract the athlete from concentrating. The football receiver needs to focus attention on the ball to catch it. The basketball shooter must be able to focus on the front or back of the rim. The baseball or softball batter must be able to concentrate on the ball.

The overly anxious athlete will not be able to focus attention on the appropriate task. The player may begin to worry about what others are thinking as attention drifts. During competition the athlete's attention becomes misdirected. The athlete may direct attention on the anticipated consequences of poor performance. "What will others think of me if I lose?" "Does my coach think I'm terrible?" "Are my friends laughing at me?" "Am I letting my teammates down?" "Will my parents be upset with me?" The athlete who has been performing poorly may also further impair his or her performance by worrying about the effectiveness of his/her technique. The more often the basketball shooter misses, the greater the worry about elbow position, wrist position, follow-through. The more often players worry about the spin of the ball or who they're supposed to block out for the rebound, the more their concentration will be misdirected and their performance will suffer. Clearly, it becomes a circular problem.

Don't Psyche Them Out

Most coaches believe the best way to prepare a team for a contest is to increase tension and arousal to its maximal level — that if athletes are not "sky high" prior to a game, they are not mentally prepared or not really interested or motivated to play. The coach seldom recognizes that the relaxed athlete is likely the most prepared and self-confident. Far too often, the coach, who is usually very nervous, regards the relaxed athlete as apathetic and unprepared for the upcoming game.

All athletes do not necessarily perform all skills most effectively at an extremely high level of arousal. Coaches want to know more and more about the level of arousal which is best for their team or for individual players. It is clear that most coaches get their teams up too high, partially because the only model available is the pro or college football coach. This is an inappropriate model for youth coaches because advanced athletes perform more effectively at a high level of arousal than beginning athletes and maximal arousal levels differ for different kinds of skills. A low level of arousal is most effective for skills requiring fine, coordinated movements, steadiness and balance, such as hitting and pitching a baseball, quarterbacking in football, serving in tennis, penalty kicks in soccer, field goal kicking in football, short iron shots and putting in golf, skating figure 8's, and archery, bowling, and fencing skills. On the other hand, sports involving mainly large muscle movements, such as blocking or tackling in football, running, wrestling, weight lifting, or swimming races, may be positively affected by high arousal levels. An intermediate level of arousal is most effective for most basketball, soccer, lacrosse, hockey and gymnastic skills.

Coaches should try to find the optimal arousal level for each athlete. In general, the athlete needs to be aroused to a level above his normal, resting state for any sports skill. When athletes are apathetic, they may need to have their arousal level increased; however, for most athletes their arousal levels are already increased at game time. Often it is difficult to differentiate between the apathetic and the overly anxious, nervous athlete. The superior coach knows each athlete personally and can tell the difference between the apathetic and the overly aroused. The inverted-U relationship between arousal and performance implies that athletes must attempt to discover their peak arousal level; anything below or above it will cause their performance to deteriorate. Veteran athletes usually know what this ideal level is, but young athletes need a great deal of help and guidance from the coach.

FIGURE 1

INVERTED-U RELATIONSHIP BETWEEN AROUSAL AND PERFORMANCE

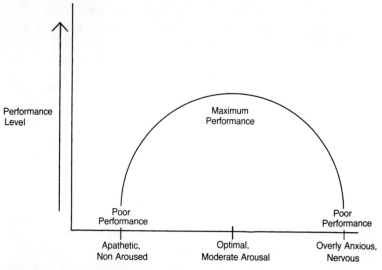

Figure 1. Arousal level.

We need to teach young athletes the importance of relaxation to increase skill performance. Young athletes can be successfully taught to relax through progressive relaxation exercises as well as through deep and slow breathing exercises.

Maximizing the Practice and Game Environment

Practice. The coach should be sure that practice sessions are designed to allow each team member to acquire new skills and build confidence. Encourage enthusiasm and avoid frustration for each athlete. Remember that young athletes develop to their potential at different ages. Avoid any emotional upset to the young athlete who might not yet be very highly skilled.

Whenever new skills are being learned, practice drills should be conducted in a relaxed atmosphere. Fans and/or parents should be discouraged from attending practices until skills have been well mastered. Competitive drills should also be excluded from practice plans until an advanced skill level has been attained.

In the initial stages of skill acquisition, young athletes should be encouraged to experiment with the skills and figure out how to perform or apply them in new situations. As they explore and attempt to perform the skills, the coach should offer feedback and encouragement to each athlete, letting the athlete know which aspects of the skill he or she is performing correctly, followed by corrections and refinements of the skills. Solving involvement of each athlete and providing an environment which maximizes success for all will eliminate anxiety and frustration which can interfere with skill development.

Occasionally athletes become bored with practice, usually when the tasks are too easy. The perceptive coach will recognize this problem and increase the complexity and difficulty of the tasks. However, practice at a skill should not cease just because the athletes have done it correctly once or twice. Continued practice in a variety of situations will insure overlearning which is helpful for skill retention, confidence and relaxation, qualities that are conducive to better performance in the game.

Competitive drill is effective for motivation after the relevant skills are well learned. At this stage, competition will be beneficial because it usually elicits the properly learned and executed skill. As the season approaches, practice sessions should begin to approximate the game situation as closely as possible. Increased levels of arousal might be induced by practice games and encouraging parents and other spectators to attend. This should prepare the athletes, get them used to an audience and make them more relaxed in the real game situation.

The emphasis should be on improvement and enjoyment in practice. Athletes should be taught that winning is important but that losing is not the end of the world. The most important point is that the athlete strives for his or her own personal goals and for team goals.

Games. The mere anticipation of an upcoming game can lead to a rather abrupt increase in anxiety and arousal levels for the young athlete and the coach. The coach may feel that his/her honor is at stake. The coach isn't actually playing the game but may feel highly aroused, and unfortunately, an uptight coach may make the athletes highly anxious. The coach must be calm on game days, for a relaxed coach can greatly help the athletes' performance. The coach who understands the importance of relaxation will be sure to impress on athletes, parents, friends and fans the value of a relaxed atmosphere.

At games, parents and fans should be encouraged to cheer and applaud not only good performance but also displays of effort. Booing and catcalls from fans should be prohibited. Parents in particular should be made aware of the detrimental effects of an overemphasis on winning. They must realize that even a sad look on their face when their child loses or performs poorly can be damaging to the young athlete. On the other hand, an environment in which there is a complete absence of stress is not ideal or realistic either. The youth sport environment should be shaped to maximize the positive physical and psychological development of the young athlete to be able to strive for a goal and accept success or failure as temporary.

Post-Game. A team meeting should be planned immediately following a game, whether it is a victory or a defeat. A victory will allow the team to share the euphoric feelings and come back down to earth. After a defeat, the meeting allows the coach and players to discuss problem areas, bright spots and what skills need continued practice. The coach should point out strengths and stress the probability of doing better the next time.

The parent's role following a contest is also crucial. Parents must be encouraged to show love and encouragement no matter how the child performs.

Conclusion

The coach of youth sports plays an important role. We must fully understand the relationship between anxiety and performance. The coach should be sure to provide an environment which allows each child to develop to his or her fullest potential.

The athlete who is taught to feel good about his/her potential will enjoy practicing and working toward improvement. We must be sure we are turning all athletes on to sport rather than turning some on and some off, depending on the way we perceive their ability. When athletes feel positive about themselves they will be motivated toward lifetime involvement in sport.

Suggestions for Further Reading

Deci. Edward. *Intrinsic Motivation*. New York: Plenum Press, 1975.

Fait, H.F. and Billing, J.E. Reassessment of the value of competition. In H. McGlynn, ed. *Issues in Physical Education and Sports.* Palo Alto, CA: National Press Books, 1974.

Nideffer. Robert M. *The Inner Athlete: Mind Plus Muscle for Winning.* New York: Thomas Crowell, 1976.

Thomas, Jerry and W. Halliwell. Personality and motivational development: Implications for children's sports. Paper presented at The Child in Sport: A Symposium on Readiness and Effects. AAHPER National Convention, Milwaukee, Wisconsin, March 31-April 1, 1976.

Management of Your Team

Chapter 6

Leo Trich, Jr.
PONY Baseball, Inc.

Understanding the Program

First, familiarize yourself as much as possible with the workings of the program and league. You may want to ask questions to help you evaluate the program. What are its goals and objectives? Does it stimulate physical and mental growth? Is it affiliated with a state or national organization or is it strictly local? What are the advantages or disadvantages of these various arrangements? And perhaps most important of all, do you feel this particular program can achieve the ideals and goals for which it strives? If you are to produce a desirable effect on young people, you must believe completely in the program.

Make every effort to cooperate with the league officials or administrators of the organization. They too are often volunteers and share your interest in helping young people. The way you address yourself to those officials and game officials (umpires, etc.) will be watched very carefully by the children you coach and their parents. Your example will influence their behavior as well.

You And Your Team

Now, for the first time, you look at your team — living, breathing, enthusiastic young people. Just as you are assessing their ability, size, behavior and personality, they, too, are formulating their opinions of you. Try to make that first encounter an easy and honest one.

Make your approach honest; don't pretend to be something you're not. Coaches are "fire and brimstone" coaches, while others are more casual. Be yourself. Young people usually soon figure out what is real and what is not.

Building a relationship takes time, so don't expect to know immediately all the right things to say or do. Take time to get to know them and let them get to know you.

In a team sport situation there is usually more than one adult supervisor. These additional coaches or assistants play an important role in the success that you, the players and the team will have. When selecting assistants, be certain they share your desire to help young people and some of your philosophy or style of coaching. When you cannot attend practice sessions or games you'll rely on your assistant coach or coaches to take charge. So that they will not totally lack experience, let them share in the duties and responsibilities of practice and game situations. It's important that they relate well with the team members. Their ability and desire to work directly and effectively with your players will be of great help to you during the season.

Organization and Practice

If practices are to accomplish all that is expected, they must be well planned. Practice time will be at a premium and therefore should be utilized to the fullest. They should also be interesting and fun. This is not to say that hard work and advocating dedication and devotion to improving one's ability should be abandoned. Do the best you can to achieve both.

Although many practice techniques wil be done on a team or group basis, often subject to time limitations, it may be worth the added effort to concentrate on youngsters who don't learn as fast as others. Taking extra time during practice may not be the answer. Because of the delay caused and in fairness to the other players, perhaps additional time before or immediately after your scheduled session will be in everyone's best interest. However, all youngsters should receive equal opportunities during regular practice periods. You should allow for individual progress while accomplishing a feeling of team effort and unity. Since no two persons are alike, it should be understood and expected, whether you're working with a two-, three- or four-year age span on any given team, that there are developmental differences among youngsters, even among those of the same age. That difference is not only in physical abilities, but in emotions and personality as well.

A very important aspect in coaching is proper encouragement and positive reinforcement at the right time. These young people for various reasons, personal ambitions, love of the sport and peer pressures, will be giving their very best, even though it may not always seem that way to you, the other players or the fans, especially after the fifth batter in a row has been walked, or the third fumble in as many carries has taken place. In almost every instance, however, that youngster will be doing his or her very best. Being too critical at such a time can be damaging to a youngster's self-confidence and desire to continue with a good attitude. A kind, understanding word can go a long way, especially from the coach. In this situation you become the most important critic of all. Constructive criticism and occasional disciplining should be done at practice sessions rather than in game situations. A "pat on the back" for good attempt is just as important as one for the game-saving play. Some youngsters will never enjoy the thrill of single-handedly winning a game or being the star pitcher, yet their desires and efforts may be just as intense. Let them know you are aware of those efforts and that they play a significant role in the overall success of the team. It takes extra time, but the benefits will more than make it worthwhile.

Safety

Always stress safety to your players. Even the most innocent horseplay can result in serious injury. The sporting goods industry has done much to improve safety equipment. Take full advantage of these protective products. In most sports, even the size of equipment is important to the well-being of your players. Batting helmet sizes, protective padding, headgears, etc., must be properly fitted.

The quality of equipment must also be examined. Saving money in the purchase of an inferior piece of gear may result in a much more valuable loss caused by injury. Instill in the youngsters a sense of respect and need for such equipment, and encourage its use.

Another aspect of safety is the facility used for the sport. Wet infields, dirty gym floors, etc., can cause serious and unnecessary injuries. Whether indoors or outside, be certain the conditions are suitable for the hard type of play achieved at a successful practice. The "big game" is not worth the loss of players by avoidable accidents.

Keep'em On Your Side

During the course of the season it will be very helpful to you and the program to establish a cooperative spirit between the players, parents, and yourself. Parents will be dedicated, loyal fans who can be valuable workers for fund-raising projects, concession stands, and transportation. Keep parents informed and involved in league or team projects.

Begin any sport with a pre-season orientation for parents. Explain the objective of the program and what will be expected of them and their youngsters. You will find them interested and appreciative.

To prevent problems later on a few points you might want to cover during your discussion with parents are: (1) Help them understand and accept the capabilities and limitations of the players. Added pressures at home created by over-expecting and perfectionist attitudes will tend to hinder the youngsters' progress. (2) Stress the importance of their "adult" behavior in the stands as spectators and after the game. Their children will be influenced by their actions. Embarrassment to the parents, players and league can be prevented if conduct is controlled. (3) During games and practice sessions, you and your coaching staff must be in control. Let it be known that "extra coaching" from parents can cause confusion and problems not only for their child, but for the entire team as well. As team leaders, your decisions must be final and respected. (4) The game, whether a win or a loss, should end with the climax of the game. Advise parents not to dwell on the mistakes or shortcomings of the game or event. The players know better than anyone else if they have erred. One word of encouragement is more beneficial than a lecture filled with criticism.

Communications between you and the parents should continue beyond this initial orientation. A constant communicative relationship with parents is essential throughout the season. Team picnics or outings are not only fine social activities, but are good for morale.

Willingness To Listen

The ability to communicate effectively with young people is a job not often thought of, but it is perhaps the most difficult responsibility to execute correctly. Their lives can be as complex and difficult as adult life.

At times you will be required to act as a sounding board and a listener. Their problems will vary from seemingly unimportant matters, such as a broken bike or the loss of a favorite glove, to problems at home or school or with a "sweetheart."

These problems are real and extremely important to them. Unfortunately, problems can even reach the magnitude of drug-taking, mental disturbances or other equally critical situations. You are not expected to have all the proper educational background or expertise to deal with those types of rare conditions, but you should be prepared. Showing concern for that individual is an important step. Depending on the severity of the problem, the parents should be alerted. Although you may not be able to help directly, references to a proper agency or someone who can help will do the most good.

Becoming involved in the personal lives of others is not something one should seek. However, if help is requested it would be unfair and against the best interest of that young person to refuse to help.

Final Thought

Teaching the fundamentals of the sport in which you are involved is only part of your overall duties. As a volunteer youth leader, there is a substantial difference in the goals and objectives you should have, compared to those of a paid athletic supervisor on a high school, college, or professional level. These youngsters are not only players on your team, but neghbors, schoolmates of your own children, and just plain frends; thus your dealings are much more intimate.

Do not try to relive your own ambitions through their efforts; always keep in mind that these youngsters have specific desires and goals of their own. Share the moments of gladness and victory, but be prepared to feel their anguish in defeat or rejection.

In some ways, your job is demanding, but if handled properly, the rewards to you as well as to the young people you serve, go far beyond financial value.

There will be times when everything seems to be going wrong. You may even come under criticism for your game strategy or for not arguing with an umpire over a close call at second. But a simple comment from one of your players like, "thanks, coach" or an unspoken expression of pride and joy in the face of a youngster who has just got his first hit or caught his first pass will erase most, if not all, the taxing experiences.

Legal Liability

Most amateur youth athletic organizations offer legal liability insurance coverage to their member leagues which protect league officers and directors in the event of legal action requiring payment for bodily injury or death, or destruction of property caused by accidents arising out of operations involved in the conduct of league activity.

Release forms or waivers signed by parents are advisable, but may not provide complete protection because (1) a parent cannot sign away the rights of a minor, and (2) in the event of serious or disabling injury to a child, a court action may award damages even though a waiver had been signed.

The responsibility of the coach, in the event of injury, is to use reasonable care and diligence in obtaining competent medical care. The seriousness of injury, particularly to the head, should not be a matter for guesswork by the amateur coach. If there is any doubt at all, the player should be examined by a physician or at a medical facility. Coaches should be sure parents or legal guardians are advised.

Accident insurance covering medical costs for injury to players, coaches and league officials is offered through organized youth leagues or local insurance agents. Many players are covered by family medical insurance plans, but be sure that all players are covered. If the league does not purchase accident coverage, it is advisable to obtain the name of the company providing insurance coverage for each player's family, each family's insurance certificate number, and the name of the family's physician. Such information should be readily available to the coach at practice sessions, games or other league activities in case a player requires hospitalization when the parents (or legal guardian) are unavailable.

Another problem involving judgment by the coach is the return of the player to practice following any serious injury. The best policy is to require a permission slip from an attending physician, or at least the parents or guardians or the player, stating the date the player may return to team activity.

Before each playing season, it is advisable, since state laws do vary, to have an insurance agent, a lawyer, or someone else, who may be similarly familiar with insurance law in your state to discuss acts which might constitute negligence on the part of the coach, and legal liability insurance in general. In the years ahead you'll see these young people from time to time. And soon they won't be quite so small as they were during that season played not so long ago. The satisfaction of helping young people, of watching their development, not merely in ability but mentally, physically and socially will be gratifying to say the least.

Many heartwarming experiences will turn into fond memories that you will enjoy and relive many times over. And when you have achieved such a technique for capturing a glimpse of the past, you will have captured a part of youth that you can keep and cherish forever.

MEDICAL CONSULTATION*

Physical Examination

All youths entering a sports program should have a thorough physical examination by a physician who is aware of the importance of the exam in preventing debilitating injuries and maintaining health. The physician should be aware of medical conditions which require further appraisal by a consultant specialist. For example, no child with a cardiac defect should be excluded from participating in a sport without a consultation with a cardiologist who is knowledgable concerning heart defects in the young.

An annual complete physical examination is not necessary for every youth. A repeat complete evaluation should be performed in a youth who has been injured or has had a significant illness between seasons or sports. For the healthy youngster, an evaluation of vital signs, especially blood pressure, should be performed annually, and a complete evaluation every other year.

In Case of Emergency

Every team should have a team physician who is present or readily available for game and practice sessions. If an injury requires immediate treatment, the family should sign a waiver permitting the team physician to care for the child.

A qualified physician should be on duty at each varsity football game and available but not necessarily present for all games where participants are under 14 years of age. The physician should be available preceding the game to evaluate any athlete's fitness to play. The physician should also be available on the field during the games to examine and perform any needed first aid procedures and to decide whether:

1. The player is capable of continued participation without increased risk of further injury or aggravation of existing injuries
2. The player should not continue to play because of the likelihood that further participation could result in aggravation of the injury or a more serious injury. If this decision is reached, the physician should:

- - - - -

*This section on Medical Consultation was written by William B. Strong, M.D., Pediatric Cardiology, Medical College of Georgia, Augusta, GA.

a. Determine if the injured athlete needs immediate referral to a hospital or other medical facility, or

b. Determine that although the athlete cannot continue to participate in the game, the injury, while demanding medical attention and further evaluation at a later time, does not justify immediate transfer to a medical facility.

At half-time and following each game, the squad should be assembled in the dressing room and the physician, in the presence of the coach, should re-check any injured athlete. Each team must remain in the dressing room until all injured athletes have been checked and properly cared for.

Athletes who are wholly or partially ambulatory may be transported to the hospital or appropriate medical facility by auto. Serious and non-ambulatory cases should be transported by ambulance.

When the athlete is sent to a hospital or other medical facility, the referring physician should call the hospital or facility and notify them that an athlete with an injury is being sent and, when possible, give the diagnosis. The physician should also notify the medical facility of the athlete's condition at the time of referral.

Recommendation Concerning Head Injuries in Football Players

Any athlete knocked unconscious during a game will be removed from the game and not allowed to return. The athlete should be checked by a physician during the game and, if necessary, immediately following the game, and if the condition justifies, the patient should be removed to a medical facility for further evaluation. Any athlete who is dazed or groggy or who has loss of memory or other symptoms of a head injury must be removed from the game and remain on the sidelines for observation by a physician for at least one quarter. The physician may keep the athlete out of the game longer if it is in the athlete's best interest. The athlete should also be evaluated immediately after the game and if the condition so justifies, be sent to a medical facility for further evaluation.

This policy which has been in effect at the high schools in Atlanta, Georgia for more than five years, has eliminated a lot of controversy as to who should or should not be allowed to return to participate following a head injury. If this recommendation is accepted by the coaches throughout youth league football, and made mandatory of this committee (Committee on Pediatric Aspects of Physical Fitness, Recreation and Sports of the American Academy of Pediatrics) a progressive step toward reducing the number of serious consequences following head injuries will have been taken.

Winning Isn't Everything Nor Is It the Only Thing!

Walter E. Cooper
University of Southern Mississippi

Players generally believe that winning is important, but not as important as *having fun*. In a recent survey, 72 percent of the players indicated they would rather play on a losing team than sit on the bench on a winning team.

Some critical questions that arise about winning and losing in youth sports programs are:

- What are the purposes and goals of youth sports programs?
- What are the problems relative to the proper emphasis on winning?
- How can a proper appraisal of performance and appreciation for sport become an integral part of programs?
- What are constructive responses to winning and losing for coaches, players and spectators?
- What about parent-child relationships in win-lose situations?
- What are some key tips on the emphasis on winning?

Joe Paterno on winning . . .

. . . We can't let people get hold of our kids and make them think they've got to win. The winning is great. You strive for it. You try to do it. You compete to win. But if we lose, we lose. I've never been in a football game where there wasn't enough glory for everybody . . . winners and losers. I think that's something we've got to keep in mind.

George Leonard in *The Ultimate Athlete*, notes:

Competition can be placed in the proper perspective, as an aid to achievement and a matter of good sportmanship. The short-term excitement and intensity created by the overblown desire to win at all costs can be replaced by a more durable excitement and intensity springing from the athletic experience itself. We may discover that sports and physical education, reformed and refurbished, may provide us with the best possible path to personal enlightenment and social transformation in this age.

James Michener, author of *Sports in America,* pleads with fathers, mothers, volunteer coaches and others to listen to knowledgeable professionals in physical education and recreation.

> *. . . They are not against rugged games for boys; they want their sons to engage in rough and tumble of childhood sports . . .*
> *BUT THEY ARE AGAINST HIGHLY STRUCTURED LEAGUES RUN BY HYPERTENSIVE ADULTS, URGED ON BY OVER-ENTHUSIASTIC FATHERS AND MOTHERS.*

Michener goes on to write,

> *I believe that children, like little animals, require play and competition in order to develop.*
> *I believe play is a major agency in civilizing infants.*
> *I believe big muscle movement helps the infant establish his balance within space in which he will henceforth operate.*
> *I believe that competition, reasonably supervised, is essential to the full making of the individual.*
> *Children should have the widest possible experience of play — there are exercises that even two-month-old infants can be given by their parents — but heavily organized competition with end-of-season championships should not be initiated before the age of twelve, if then.*

I must relate a personal story involving my eight-year-old son Patrick, who has had two years of "T" ball baseball. In Hattiesburg, Mississippi, all youngsters who come out are placed on a team, "uniforms" are t-shirts and caps, — there are no practices or formal coaching, and no standings are kept during the six-week, one-game-a-week schedule. All went well for Patrick and his teammates during their first year of six wins and no losses. Patrick asked me many questions about rules, from tagging up after fly balls which was very confusing, to force-outs on bases. We pitched together, bunted, hit and so on — a very constructive experience.

The second year began well, with a win, but then two losses. Each time, my boy hung his head and trudged off the field with tears in his eyes. I told him, "You've won maybe more than your share, now you're learning to lose. It doesn't feel good and shouldn't, but you'll get over it. You tried hard — you did your best." Within five minutes he had recovered and went down the street for more play.

I hope he can keep sports in this perspective — prepare well, do the best he can, and accept the results.

Purposes and Goals of Youth in Sports

Havighurst, in *Developmental Levels of Play* (1976), describes some of the problems of competition for youth in our society:

> *Playing to win, in a competition, enhances both skills and strategy. The competition provides motivation to practice and improve skills, and it also encourages careful planning of strategy to win. Although some people decry competition, this writer sees it as a highly valuable and desirable experience in the lives of growing youth, as long as it is regulated and spread out over enough activities so that practically every youth can achieve some degree of success in some area or areas of competition.*
>
> *Therefore the activities in which competition takes place should be planned and administered so as to maximize opportunity for success in some areas. This suggests the importance of a wide variety of activities in which competition functions — not only in athletics, but also in dramatics, music, scientific experiments, debate, chess, foreign language facility, the writing of short stories, poetry, etc.*

Havighurst's model, "Developmental Levels of Play," could be quite helpful in organizing and supervising competitive situations for youth (see Figure 1).

101

This model relates key developmental concerns across age levels. Recreation and school professionals in physical education and coaching should work with volunteer groups in understanding developmental concerns in organizing and supervising youth sports programs.

FIGURE 1

Age	Forms and Functions of Play	
Birth to 5	Self-initiated. Exploration of body and immediate surroundings. Sensory basis for building concepts of physical reality.	
5 to 14	Social Play	Individual Play
	Getting along with peers Social maturation	Reading for pleasure Playing with musical instruments Developing skills in physical games and activities
		Games of Skill and Strategy
12 to 20		Beginning of competition Development of strategy Acquiring more mature moral judgement through working out rules for games
	Team Games	
	Complex strategy	Reading contributes to intellectual and social maturity
	Danger from over-developed competition	

Figure 1. Developmental levels of play, Havighurst (1976).

Most authorities agree that youth sports leaders should:
- At ages up to about 12 years, emphasize development of basic skills, learning rules and strategies, and developing an appreciation for participation.
- Emphasize individual and team performance rather than winning the contest.
- Gradually develop the emphasis on winning championships rather than superimpose the pro and college model on young kids.
- Carefully select coaches and provide training programs to overcome concerns in overall development, as well as specific sports skills.
- Familiarize parents with the goals of the program and their constructive role.
- *Always* respect the dignity of every participant. Let the *child* make the choice!
- Allow every participant to experience success.
- Help youngsters understand the feelings of winning and losing by appraisal after all contests.
- Consider activities and contests in which the primary goal is cooperation rather than competition.
- Understand the role that youth sports programs can play in the development of self-understanding (positive self-concept).
- Provide alternative activities so that one activity doesn't require all available free time.
- Provide for the younger participants (up through age 12, maybe 15) the opportunity to participate — no cuts!

PEANUTS®   Release Week of November 26 to December 1, 1973   By Charles M. Schulz

© 1973, United Features Syndicate, Inc.

It is vitally important that these or similar goals be discussed and drafted in writing for the training of coaches and the orientation of parents. Constructive competitive sports programs for youth do not occur by chance!

In a recent study of 289 Little League foolball players, ages 9 to 15, it was revealed that players generally liked their coaches, but did not want them to:

- yell a lot
- become angry over a loss
- be too tough
- smoke and swear
- always want to win
  The values the players felt they received were:
- getting in shape
- knowing the game better
- learning to work with others
- sportsmanship
- forming friendships
- having fun

This would seem to be fairly typical of youngsters, so why don't we listen to the kids?

Stephen Kaufman wrote recently, "In triumph or in defeat, a good job is still a good job."

"Good time?" Kaufman wrote, "My father once screamed at me during one of my six little league baseball seasons, 'Win your games then you'll have a good time.' " Kaufman continues:

. . .And so the boy is hustled into the appropriate little league program, where emphasis is placed on winning rather than:

- enjoyment of participation
- the satisfaction of physical exercise
- the pleasure of working up a sweat
- getting in shape
- having a good time.

Appraising Results for Players and Parents

A proper perspective on winning and losing is a very important component of successfully organizing and supervising competitive youth sports programs. Rainer Martens, a sports psychologist at the University of Illinois, notes:

The crux of the problem then is knowing when winning is over-emphasized. Actually it is not as difficult as it may appear to detect the win-at-all costs philosophy. We can with some accuracy infer coaches' motives by observing their behaviors..

- *when coaches play injured youngsters*
- *when they leave players sitting on the bench the entire season, and*
- *when they routinize practice so that it becomes a complete bore.*

Over-Emphasis Is Indicated: When in the frantic race to be first, the developmental objectives blur into the background, winning is out-of-bounds.

Terry Orlick of the University of Winnipeg says that in youth sports, rewards depend on the defeat of others and emphasis always seems to be placed on some numerical outcome. He writes, "Games of acceptance must replace games of rejection."

He also suggests that a basic problem in most games and sports is that two or more people or teams want what only one can have (i.e , the ball or the victory).

Thus it becomes a question of how far each will go in order to get the ball or to achieve the victory . . . It also becomes a question of how one reacts when they do not get the ball or when they do not achieve the scoreboard victory.

The coach of youth must realize there is more to the athletic contest than who wins or loses (outcome) and that appraisal of performance during and after the contest is needed.

The 'Outcome-Performance' Model, suggested by Martens, offers the volunteer coach a means of understanding and organizing himself for appraisal of performance, individual and team, during and after competition (See Figure 2).

The coach should continually appraise strong and weak points of performance. A 'chart of comments' could easily be kept during the game to be used in the after-the-game team meeting and later practices. Thus the 'outcome' of the contest diminishes in importance as improvement in skill and behavior during the contest is constantly referred to.

Comparing oneself with others becomes very important to children in grades four, five, or six. To excel in motor skills is one of the most prized abilities of children.

The evaluation from significant others, e.g., parents, peers, and coaches is vitally important to children. Examples include:

- Parental pride and approval after a touchdown and disapproval after a fumble
- Cues elicited by teammates when superior or inferior players come up to bat in critical situations. Teammates praise or

FIGURE 2

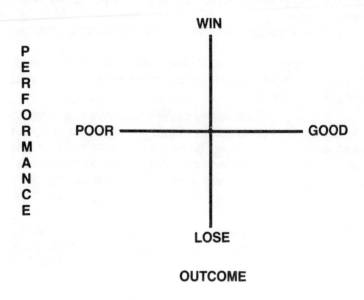

Figure 2. Win/lose — performance matrix. Martens (1971).

rebuke, opponents sometimes congratulate or ridicule and spectators ofter cheer or jeer.
• Assessment by coaches of players in picking the team, choosing who starts and who substitutes, and selecting all-star candidates.

Social evaluation constantly indicates to the child whether he or she is a winner or loser — a success or a failure! Therefore, coaches, parents and peers must be aware of the impact they have on a players subsequent understanding and acceptance of him/herself.

Win or Lose, Why?

Glen Roberts of the University of Illinois, has related winning and losing in competitive youth sport to the attribution theory in psychology. This theory, which has been labeled the "common sense" approach, asks, how do people make sense out of our complex world?

People seem to perceive four major causes of winning or losing:

1. Ability
2. Effort
3. Task Difficulty
4. Luck

Successes or failures may be attributed to internal controls (ability or effort); while others might be determined by external factors (the difficulty of the task or luck).

Someone suggested that in attribution theory, it's not whether you win or lose, but where you place the credit or blame. A study by Roberts of 200 Little League baseball players deals with the causal attributions children make when they win or lose a game. Teams which consistently won credited the successes to their ability and did not consider it diminished when they lost. Teams which consistently lost attributed their losses to poor ability. Players on winning teams that lost attributed high effort to themselves, but low effort to other team members.

Roberts has written:

Teams which consistently lost were more likely to attribute success to unstable factors . . . thus losing teams did not expect that winning a game would insure success in the future. Previously successful teams, on the other hand, attributed failure to unstable factors, thus expecting to win in the future . . .

Unfortunately, young athletes who continually lose, feel that the outcome of the game is beyond their personal control and may eventually drop out of the activity, possibly even resort to mal-adaptive behavior. These "perennial losers" may exhibit learned helplessness and not be able to perceive the success-effort relationship.

Can coaches help youth understand the success-effort relationship? Yes, if we organize so that every child, particularly under about 15 years of age, experiences some successes. How can we do this?

Try putting all players back in the pot after five games and randomly assign them to teams, and repeat this after 10 games. Then keep win×loss records for coaches (if they still want them)! The coach who now goes 15 wins, no losses, has done one heck of a teaching job. The coach with zero wins and 15 losses may want to seek fulfillment elsewhere.

Parents Can Make a Difference

Parents and coaches can make a world of difference as to whether the competitive experience is constructive or destructive!

Bernard Mackler, a well-respected psychologist, wrote in a sensitive article on youth sports, ". . . After viewing a game in which parents screamed 'kill the umpire' and 'stick it in his ear,' I finally decided that we teach them that winning is everything and that being ugly and violent is acceptable."

And even Erma Bombeck has had a say in her own unique way about youth sports emphasis:

On the way home they tried to comfort me. "Hey, it's just a championship game where you either bring honor to your team or humiliate them. Don't sweat it. You almost gave your best. Of course in that second set, you stood there like you were waiting for a city bus . . ."

"And you could have gotten that corner shot if you'd had a racket back in time, but what the heck . . .Hey, your opponent had 30 pounds on you. We're just going to have to get you into better shape. We'll get it all together before next week's match. Besides, you had a wonderful time didn't you?"

I woke up in a cold sweat. What a lousy dream. It was a dream, wasn't it? What am I saying? Of course it was. I mean, how many people push their mothers into organized sports? Or children, for that matter. (Hattiesburg American, April 28, 1977).

Tips from Former Youth Athletes

In an issue of *The Christian Athlete* (November 1976) presenting results from a poll of former youth league athletes, some of the respondents said the following in regard to changes they would make in youth sports:

. . . Too much attention put on 'winning at any cost' instead of simply playing your best and being a good sport. Somehow I would like to see the pressure of winning taken off the backs of young kids today.

* * * *

Work on the sport, not on winning.

* * * *

I would like to take all the emphasis off winning and remove the all-star games.

Less emphasis on winning since losing players can get discouraged before they really understand winning and losing.

*   *   *   *

I would like to see more coaches interested in the kids rather than just winning.

*   *   *   *

Change the winning thing. Like you have to win. Smile or laugh a little.

*   *   *   *

Winning Isn't Everything

Many leaders in youth sports, including Arthur Esslinger, for many years a member of the board of directors of Little League Baseball, have emphasized the potential constructive and/or destructive forces possible through involvement in competitive sport. Esslinger said,

> *The heart of Little League Baseball is what happens between the manager and boy. It is your manager more than any other single individual who makes your program a success or failure. He controls the situation in which the players may be benefited or harmed. We have all seen managers who exerted a wonderful influence upon their boys — an influence which was as fine an educational experience as any lad might undergo. Unfortunately we have also observed a few managers who were a menace to children.*

Can we really do anything to modify programs — to create new models — to revamp the organization and supervision of competitive youth sports programs? Can we develop a proper perspective on winning and losing and integrate this into program development? Yes, we can!

When the National Junior Tennis League held its 1975 national finals at Forest Hills, the league officials did not like what they saw — a "must win" attitude. "It turned into a highly emotional, unnecessarily pressure-filled experience. When the stakes get too high, the kids' game becomes an adult game. It's just not good for them." So the league subsequently has abolished its national

TANK McNAMARA   **by Jeff Millar & Bill Hinds**

TANK McNAMARA   **by Jeff Millar & Bill Hinds**

Copyright 1977, Universal Press Syndicate

championships and decided to keep competition on local and regional levels. But even there it will de-ephasize; no regional team champions will be designated. "What it will amount to," said Frank Hannah, league executive administrator, "is that players from different cities will have an opportunity to meet new people. Not only will they play tennis for fun, but they'll also play softball and swim, and . . . just have a good time!"

Community Coordinating Council

One suggestion by Bryant Cratty for improving the organization and supervision of youth sport was a community coordinating council! Preliminary results from a local effort in Hattisburg, Mississippi of parent clinics, civic club presentations, and assistance in programs appears to be having a constructive effect. The approach is to promote guidelines for sound development of children and youth through competitive sport experiences.

Cratty also noted that in California, youth soccer league commissioners and coaches were observed who had organized and supervised programs with development of knowledge about rules and strategies and basic skill as the primary goals. Parents and participants cooperated with the coaches to produce more suc-

110

cessful programs. However, where winning of championships was the primary goal, from the top level down, there was lack of cooperation and aggression among players, parents, coaches and officials. This underlines the major need for organization and supervision of programs based on sound developmental guidelines.

The more we make sports a life-and-death matter, and the more we concentrate on a youngster's needing to win or succeed in order to feel worthwhile, the more we will undermine the contribution that sports can make. Let's eliminate the grandiosity of sports and recognize what it should offer to 99 percent of those who participate: healthy recreation in an environment where a child can have fun while developing physical skills and emotional maturity in a positive interaction with other children.

Let's teach young athletes the fundamentals, talk to them about their batting average and field goal percentages, and take pride in their triumphs. But let's not neglect or abuse their motivations and emotions. Let's not forget that when they pull on a uniform, they are still children, not miniature adults. (Thomas Tutko and William Bruns, in their book *Winning is Everything and Other American Myths*).

Appendix

A. Coach and Program Self Inventory

(Material Selected from Chapters in the *Youth Sports Guide*)

Directions for Use of Youth Sports Inventory

As you read through and respond to the Inventory, ask yourself whether you understand and apply the principles and concepts involved. The information in the Inventory was selected from the research available in the field as portrayed in the chapters of this *Guide*. If you do not understand a concept, refer back to the designated chapter for further information.

Go through the Inventory and respond relative to your true feelings about the statements. This is a SELF INVENTORY for your own improvement in developing programs and working with kids.

	Response Mode					
Statements	Strongly Disagree	Disagree	Don't Know	Agree	Strongly Agree	**Comments**
1.						
2.						
3.						
4.						
5.						
6.						
7.						

Coach and Program Self Inventory

Chapter 1, Coaching Roles and Relationships (Smoll, Smith, Curtis, pp. 6-23)

1. Whether the positive potential of programs is realized depends upon how programs are organized and supervised.

2. By creating a psychologically healthy situation, all children can be winners regardless of won-lost records.

3. As a coach, you can provide the child experiences which help lead to a happy, productive, and well-adjusted life.

4. Most youth sports programs are oriented toward providing a healthy recreational and social learning experience for kids.

5. It is all too easy for coaches to get caught up in the "winning is everything" philosophy.

6. In many instances, winning becomes more important for the coach than it is for the player.

7. Winning will take care of itself within the limits of players' talents, if the coach helps them develop their athletic *abilities*.

8. While happy players don't always win, they need never lose.

9. Enjoyment of relating to a coach and teammates, feeling better about themselves, improving skills, and looking forward to further sports participation are valid goals for youth sports programs.

10. Your players will learn as much from what you do as from what you say.

11. Treating officials with respect and tolerance for mistakes will assist players in acting in a dignified manner.

12. Successful coaches are those who can help each player achieve his or her full potential.

13. Each coach should provide a valuable athletic and social growth experience for the players.

14. The toughest part of coaching is getting what you want to teach across to the kids, gaining their respect, and making them feel glad that they played for you.

15. You should create a good learning situation so that the kids acquire the skills you are trying to teach them.

16. You should create an enjoyable interpersonal situation where your players relate well to one another and to you.

17. You want to create a setting or an atmosphere in which your players will develop positive personality characteristics.

18. As a coach, you are trying to increase certain desired behaviors on the part of your players and decrease undesirable behaviors.

19. The positive approach to coaching is characterized by liberal use of reward and encouragement.

20. You should have realistic expectations and consistently reward players when they succeed in meeting them.

21. Reward effort as much as you do results.

22. Players have complete control over how much effort they make; they have only limited control over the outcome of their efforts.

23. Coaches should never use a sarcastic or degrading manner.

24. Encouragement can become contagious and aid in building team unity.

25. If you manage things right, mistakes can provide a golden opportunity to provide corrective instruction.

26. In corrective instruction, emphasize not the mistake but the good things that will happen if the player follows your instruction.

27. Mistakes have a positive side; they provide information we need to help improve performance.

28. Use a positive approach to instruction rather than punishment in any form.

29. Fear of failure can be the athlete's worst enemy.

30. Many of a coach's problems involve maintaining discipline during practices and games.

31. Kids seem to want clearly defined limits and structure.

32. Kids who have a hand in formulating rules evidence more of a commitment to live by them.

33. If a rule previously agreed upon is broken, a player has simply broken a team rule and must automatically pay the penalty — this

helps build personal accountability with the responsibility on the individual.

34. Using beneficial physical activities (running laps or doing pushups) as punishment may cause such activities to become adversive.

35. Participation should be viewed as a learning situation (rather than competitive) where you're going to help the kids develop their abilities.

36. A coach should emphasize the good things that will happen if you do it right rather than focusing on the bad things that will occur if you don't.

37. A coach should constantly ask him or herself what has been communicated to the players and whether the communication is effective.

Chapter 2, Characteristics of the Young Athlete (Rarick and Seefeldt, pp. 24-44)

38. The coach who is thoroughly acquainted with growth characteristics of the players should have a realistic outlook on thier performance capabilities.

39. The difference in ability level of young athletes is often a result of different maturational levels.

40. It is not unusual for differences in rate of maturity to exceed five years within one chronological age.

41. The rate at which children mature is closely related to their body size.

42. Girls are nearer their final body size at any age because they mature at a faster rate than boys.

43. Evidence indicates exercise can be both beneficial and detrimental to physical growth, depending upon the conditions under which it takes place.

44. Muscles, bones and nervous tissue must be subjected to activity if they are to reach their potential for development.

45. Any repetitive activity (throwing) that results in discomfort to the exercised body part is a source of undue stress.

46. Throwing a baseball has been shown to increase the rate of maturation of the throwing arm and cause marked changes in the elbow joint at the point where the greatest stress was applied.

47. Muscle cells enlarge as a result of stress.

48. Weight training for young athletes is questionable because of inefficiency of increasing muscle tissue prior to puberty and the possible detrimental effects that overloading joints may have on the ends of the long bones.

49. The use of activity to control weight is an important side effect of youth sports.

50. The more lasting effects of regularly repeated exercises result in what is known as a training effect and causes the player to respond with greater ease.

51. The cardio-respiratory (heart and lungs) adjustments are perhaps the most dramatic and readily discernible adjustments the body makes to the demands of exercise.

52. The coach should be aware that the working capacity of the young child is substantially less than that of adolescents.

53. Care must be taken that the water lost in sweating is replaced during the course of exercise by equivalent amounts of water.

54. Care should be taken that children are not permitted to engage in heavy exercise under hot, humid conditions.

55. Perhaps the most striking functional adaptations that come with training occur in the neuromuscular system and the heart.

56. The kind of strength that is developed tends to be closely associated with the training procedures that are followed.

57. The coach should be knowledgeable about the kind of strength the specific sport requires and use strengthening exercises that simulate the movements required in the sport.

58. The greatest response to strength training has been observed in the ages 12 to 15 years.

59. Athletes in early adolescence may not be as strong as their size would suggest.

60. Boys on the average are stronger than girls from 8 to 18 years of age.

61. After 13 years of age, males show a marked spurt in strength development, much greater than that shown by females.

62. With advancing age (13-18) there is a greater ability on the part of the body to mobilize and utilize the available muscle strength through improved muscle coordination that comes from experience.

63. Endurance activities may throw excessive demands on the heart of children and early adolescents.

64. Children do seem to respond favorably to endurance type activities, provided caution is exercised in medical screening and training procedures.

65. The greatest concern for the physical well-being of youth is the vulnerability of the immature skeleton to irreparable injury.

66. "Little Leaguers elbow," so named because it is most frequently seen in young baseball players, is a structural problem associated with youth sports programs.

67. Because of the stress placed on the elbow by pitching, players 14 years and below should be permitted to pitch only a few innings per game and curve ball pitching should be banned.

68. The best insurance against permanent injury is sensible decisions regarding appropriate sports for those under 14 years, proper conditioning, and provision of protective equipment.

69. There is little evidence to support the use of special foods or diets to enhance the performance of young athletes.

70. The value of extensive warmup prior to competition is questionable.

71. The use of highly structured training programs may be viewed as work rather than play by the child.

72. The coach should recognize that variations must be included in training sessions if motivation is to remain high.

73. The coach must recognize that individuals differ markedly in their ability to cope with stressful situations.

74. Inducing strong psychological stress in young athletes as a

way to enhance performance is not apt to succeed and at best is a questionable practice.

75. Refinements in movement patterns which underlie basic skills come with maturation and practice.

76. Young athletes need specific direction (verbal or demonstration) from coaches to correct mistakes when performance has been faulty.

77. Performance measures for females tend to stabilize at puberty, while those of males show a steady increase of proficiency into adulthood.

Chapter 3, Different Strokes for Different Folks: Teaching Skills to Kids (Singer, pp. 45-62)

78. The learning of specific sports skills will be hindered:
   (a) The more the child is developmentally immature
   (b) The more difficult the activity
   (c) The more restricted the child's previous experiences

79. Activities should be modified to the appropriate maturational level of children.

80. Children should be encouraged to develop basic and fundamental movement patterns prior to specialized sports skill training.

81. The coach must decide on some techniques for communicating with athletes as to what it is they are to accomplish.

82. Observation and modeling techniques should be used, especially with younger athletes.

83. Coaches should assist players in learning how to evaluate their present capabilities so they can assess personal improvement and establish realistic objectives for themselves.

84. The coach must provide cues for the players to adjust their behavior and should not assume the athlete can adjust to verbal cues alone — show them!

85. The coach should create many learning situations that are enjoyable as well as productive.

86. All players need to be encouraged to think, analyze and problem solve so as to anticipate and make correct decisions during competition.

87. Coaches should praise, encourage and look for good in spite of a loss in competition.

88. Kids naturally love to play, take risks, self-evaluate, overcome challenges, and do many of the things associated with good sports programs.

89. Many kids seem to participate in sport for the acquisition of rewards rather than for the more ideal values usually associated with athletic experiences.

90. For kids who are already intrinsically motivated to participate, rewards will do little to help and in fact may do more harm than good.

91. Rewards may change the source of motivation from playing for enjoyment and wanting to develop sports skills, to looking forward to some prize as an outcome of victory.

92. Being too excitable or anxious is likely to cause a breakdown in any coordinated effort; learning is impaired as is performance.

93. There is an optimal level of emotions, or arousal, for each kid for each activity.

94. Feelings play a great role in how we learn and perform.

95. Some activities can produce fear — fear blocks learning.

96. The coach should modify practice techniques to show young athletes understanding and sympathy when needed.

97. The child must be able to practice correctly and sufficiently if performance is to improve measurably.

98. Practice of correct movements requires the presence of adequate physical capabilities (level of fitness).

99. A good coaching technique is to show the learners the relationship between previously learned movements and presently introduced ones.

100. A wide range of movement experience in early childhood should facilitate the acquisition of specific athletic skills.

101. The coach should maintain a personal record for each athlete, considering as many factors as possible.

102. The coach must be sensitive to differences in kids and provide individual instruction and counsel where possible.

103. Thinking through the act or mental rehearsal helps to improve retention of motor skills.

104. Coaches should help kids identify the most important cue or cues in different situations and focus on them.

105. Players should be helped by coaches to anticipate certain things happening.

106. A kid who is superior in one sport may not be as effective in another sport.

107. A kid will not improve without knowledge about his performance and results of that performance.

108. Telling a kid how he did provides guidance for later action.

109. Though it may be frustrating at first to practice a skill under both speed and accuracy conditions, this may be the best approach in the long run.

Chapter 4, Shaping Up for Competition (Byrd, pp. 63-73)

110. The younger the athlete, the more stress you should put on technique and skill at the expense of conditioning.

111. Getting in shape is not as important for the younger child who is just learning the basics.

112. The different components of physical fitness required, e.g. flexibility, strength, endurance, speed, power, etc. vary depending on the specific activity.

113. The need for efficiency in an athletic contest dictates that you should aim training at meeting the special demands of the specific sport.

114. The coach should select conditioning activities as closely related to the sport as possible.

115. Athletes may differ greatly in their physical response to conditioning, some may increase by leaps and bounds, and others get little or no benefit.

116. If a child simply doesn't have the raw materials with which to work, no amount of coaching will make him/her an outstanding athlete.

117. The coach's role is critical in encouraging any child toward reaching his potential.

118. Proper nutrition is critical to the young athlete and a balanced diet with foods from the four basic groups is essential.

119. The growing young athlete has special requirements in the protein area which should be recognized.

120. The coach of young athletes should spend some time emphasizing the fundamentals of nutrition and how proper nutrition might affect performance.

121. The practice of losing weight to participate in a given classification is recognized as an unhealthy approach with many potentially ill effects.

122. Generally, the best and most efficient athletes are lean.

123. The athlete should allow about two hours between eating and playing.

124. The coaches' primary concern in cold exposure should be the prevention of injuries.

125. With the young athlete, you should never allow play or practice without adequate warmup.

126. Evaporation of sweat is the primary means of ridding the body of the excess heat produced by muscular activity.

127. Obese children have built-in insulation in their fat and are therefore more sensitive to heat stress.

128. High humidity adds to the problem of heat exposure because it hinders the evaporation of sweat needed for cooling the body.

129. It is doubtful that there is any good reason to subject children to heat stress levels which require the taking of salt tablets.

130. Every child should not only have free access to water at any time, but should be positively encouraged to drink before, during, and after activity.

131. Practice and games should, if possible, be scheduled in early morning or in the evening after sunset if environmental conditions so dictate.

132. The decision to play or practice in inclement weather should rest solely on the welfare of the child.

133. Physical exams should be compulsory for the young athlete.

134. If an injury is serious enough to necessitate the removal of a player from the game, you should not gamble by returning a boy or girl to competition without referral to a physician.

135. Never take a player's complaints lightly, some congenital defects may show up only during the stress of practice or play.

Chapter 5, Getting Them Up, Not Up Tight (Bunker and Rotella, pp.74-87)

136. The coach should be careful to turn all athletes on to sport rather than allow the coach's perception of the child's ability to turn some on and some off.

137. When a coach is a positive and confident individual, the athletes are likely to take on these characteristics.

138. In achieving to the best of his/her ability, the athlete must have proper mental attitude and emotional control.

139. Most participants in youth sports usually enter the programs highly motivated to listen to the coach, learn and improve their skills.

140. The coach must emphasize the positive rather than negative aspects of each individual's performance.

141. Participants should leave practice sessions with feelings of pride rather than shame.

142. Those athletes who believe they are talented will often perform as if they are, a self-fulfilling prophecy.

143. What the athletes believe about themselves is often more important than the ability each individual actually has.

144. An abundance of criticism will cause a child to lose confidence in his or her ability and therefore lower aspiration.

145. It is critical that the coach find ways to make all children feel good about themselves.

146. It would be anticipated that the extrinsically motivated child (plays for rewards primarily) would withdraw from participating if the rewards were eliminated.

147. Lifelong performance and enjoyment are more important than temporary goals.

148. Rewards given for quality of performance usually result in an increase in intrinsic motivation (self-generated).

149. If the coach assists each athlete in reaching his maximal potential, it would appear quite effective to make it possible for each child to receive an award.

150. The coach should assist each athlete in setting individual goals which must be attained in order to earn the desired award.

151. A sport contest is not the relaxing and always enjoyable activity so frequently claimed.

152. Many kids in contests behave in a quite different manner from which they would normally behave when not engaged in sports.

153. The emotional involvement makes sports so attractive and at the same time so frustrating and upsetting to so many youngsters.

154. Sports, by their very nature, contain many elements which are likely to produce anxiety.

155. Much anxiety is produced due to concern over effectiveness of strategies.

156. The outcome of any sport contest may be influenced to varying degrees by good or bad "breaks."

157. Good and bad breaks will, by the law of average, eventually even out.

158. Bad luck accounts for many losses, but wins are usually because we worked harder!

159. Because sport holds a respected position in today's world, children may establish unrealistic expectations.

160. The existing system of rewards and punishment may attract many kids to sport but also may cause many children to fear failing — a major procedure of anxiety.

161. The emphasis placed on winning and the very nature of competitive activity can cause young athletes to create a great deal of stress within themselves.

162. The overly anxious athlete will not usually react in the appropriate manner.

163. Many coaches believe the best way to prepare a team for a contest is to increase tension and arousal to maximal levels.

164. The relaxed athlete is most likely the prepared and fully confident athlete.

165. All athletes do not necessarily perform all skills most effectively when their level of arousal is extremely high.

166. Coaches should direct their efforts toward finding the optimal arousal level for each athlete.

167. Coaches should be concerned with relaxing players, rather than exciting them, in most sport situations.

168. It has been found for any sport skill, the athlete needs to be aroused to a level above his normal resting state.

169. The superior coach is the one who knows each athlete on a personal basis and can tell the difference between the apathetic and the overly aroused.

170. All athletes need to be motivated to discover their optimal level of arousal in order to produce their best performance.

171. The coach should teach the young athlete the importance of relaxation to increase skill performance.

172. Practice sessions should be designed so as to allow each team member to acquire new skills and build confidence.

173. Fans and parents should be discouraged from attending practices, as an audience can have a very detrimental impact on the learning of new skills.

174. In the initial stages of skill acquisition, the young athlete should be encouraged to experiment and figure out independently how to perform or apply the skills in new situations.

175. The athlete should be told which aspects of the skill he/she is performing correctly, followed by corrections and refinements of the skills.

176. The coach should recognize when athletes become bored and increase the complexity and difficulty of tasks to be practiced.

177. Continued practice in a variety of situations will insure over-

learning which will greatly aid in skill retention, confidence and relaxation.

178. Competitive drill activities may be effectively utilized for motivation once the skills needed are well learned.

179. As the season approaches, practice sessions should begin to approximate as closely as possible the game situation.

180. Practice games will prepare athletes and allow them to become accustomed to an audience and possibly aid in becoming more relaxed for the real game situation.

181. In practice, emphasis should be placed on improvement and enjoyment.

182. A nervous or highly aroused coach may cause the athletes to become highly anxious.

Chapter 6, Management of Your Team   (Trich, pp. 88-97)

183. The young athlete, for various reasons — personal, ambitions, love of sport, peer pressure, etc., is usually trying to do his/her best.

184. Emphasize safety: even the most innocent "horseplay" can result in serious injury.

185. The coach should consider safety equipment carefully and take full advantage of protective products.

186. The coach has the responsibility of creating a cooperative spirit among players, parents and officials.

187. The coach should orient parents relative to proper behavior at practice sessions, games, etc. and help create reasonable expectations.

188. One word of encouragement is more beneficial than a lecture filled with criticism.

189. Keeping a constant communicative relationship with parents is essential throughout a season.

190. The coach should be prepared, at times, to act as a sounding board and a listener.

191. The coach must be careful not to try to relive his or her own ambitions through the players' efforts.

192. Coaching young kids offers the opportunity for many enjoyable memories that one can cherish forever.

193. A parent release waiver form though advisable may not provide complete protection relative to liability.

194. The responsibility of the coach, in the event of injury, is to use reasonable care and diligence in obtaining competent medical care.

195. If there is any doubt as to the seriousness of injury, the procedure should be to have the player examined by a physician.

196. The coach should be sure that all players are adequately covered by accident and/or medical insurance.

197. In the case of a child returning to participation from serious injury, a permission slip from the attending physician should be required.

198. The coach should be thoroughly familiar with what circumstances might constitute negligence in supervising the team's activities.

Chapter 7, Winning Isn't Everything Nor Is It The Only Thing (Cooper, pp. 98-111)

199. Parents and fans should be encouraged to cheer and applaud not only good performance but also displays of effort on either team.

200. Booing and catcalls should not be allowed in any case..

201. The coach should help parents realize that a sad look on their face when a child loses or performs poorly can be very damaging to the young athlete.

202. The youth sport environment should be so shaped as to maximize the positive physical and psychological development of the young athlete to be able to strive for a goal and be able to accept either success or failure as a temporary state.

203. Immediately following the game, whether it is a victory or defeat, there should be a team meeting.

204. The coach, in the post game meeting, should point out strengths and weaknesses in performance as well as discuss the outcome.

205. Parents should be encouraged to show love and encouragement no matter how well or poorly the child performs.

206. The athlete who is taught to feel good about his/her potential will enjoy practicing and working toward improvement.

207. When athletes feel positive about themselves, they will be motivated toward lifetime involvement in sport.

B. Bibliography

Albinson, J.G. and Andrew, G.M. *Child in Sport and Physical Activity.* Baltimore: University Park Press, 1976.

The most authoritative reference on youth sports yet to be published. It is actually the proceedings from a national conference workshop held at Queens University, Kingston, Ontario, Canada.

American Alliance for Health, Physical Education, and Recreation, *Coaches' Manual.* Washington, DC: the Alliance, 1975.

AAHPER, *Desirable Athletic Competition for Children of Elementary School Age.* Washington, DC: the Alliance, 1968.

A policy statement on competitive athletics for children of elementary school age that has been approved by the American Academy of Pediatrics; the American Medical Association Committee on Medical Aspects of Sports; the Society of State Directors of Health, Physical Education, and Recreation; and AAHPER. Revised edition of this publication should be available in early 1978.

AAHPER, *Drugs and the Coach.* Washington, DC: the Alliance, 1977.

AAHPER, *Nutrition for Athletes: A Handbook for Coaches.* Washington, DC: the Alliance, 1971.

AAHPER, *What Research Tells the Coach About Baseball.* Washington, DC: the Alliance, 1971.

AAHPER, *What Research Tells the Coach About Distance Running.* Washington, DC: the Alliance, 1968.

AAHPER, *What Research Tells the Coach About Football.* Washington, DC: the Alliance, 1973.

AAHPER, *What Research Tells the Coach About Sprinting.* Washington, DC: the Alliance, 1974.

AAHPER, *What Research Tells the Coach About Swimming.* Washington, DC: the Alliance, 1967.

AAHPER, *What Research Tells the Coach About Tennis.* Washington, DC: the Alliance, 1975.

Athletic Institute. "Coaching Youth League Sports" Series. North Palm Beach, Florida, 1977.

An excellent series of manuals for players and coaches. Materials are available for baseball, basketball, football, ice hockey and soccer.

The Christian Athlete. "Youth League Sports." Part 1, Nov. 1976, vol. 20, no. 8. Part 2, Dec. 1976, vol. 20, no. 9. Kansas City, Missouri.

Two issues that focus on youth sport concerns and present excellent materials that vary from the research level of Rainer Martens' "A Den of Iniquity or a Land of Promise" to views from coaches and athletes. Very supportive of constructive approaches to organizing and supervising programs.

Cratty, Bryant. *Children and Youth In Competitive Sport.* Freeport, NY: Educational Activities, Inc., 1974.

Excellent summary of concerns about children and youth in sport. Good suggestions on conditioning and leadership training.

Griffin, Leon and Henschen, Keith. "Attitudes toward and values of little league football competition." *UpDate* (AAHPER newsletter), June 1976.

One of the few surveys in which kids' opinions are actually considered as well as those of parents and coaches. Most interesting finding was that 72 percent of the players indicated they would rather play on a losing team than sit on the bench of a winning team.

Harris, Paul E., Jr. *Fair or Foul, Soccer!, Goal!* and *The Little Book of Soccer.* Manhattan Beach, CA: Soccer for Americans, 1977.

Paul E. Harris, Jr., director of officiating for the American Youth Soccer Organization, is one of the most active soccer writers in America. Harris has written a book on soccer for parents, one for youth, one for referees, and one for coaches.

Leonard, George. *The Ultimate Athlete.* New York: Viking, 1976.

Encourages each reader to seek out the "ultimate athlete" which lies within. Presented in a way that makes one want to seek self-realization through physical activity.

Little League Baseball. Williamsport, Pennsylvania.

Little League Baseball has developed some excellent material for coaches, league administrators and parents. Much of this material is as appropriate for other youth sports as it is for little league baseball. Pamphlets that all coaches and parents would find meaningful are *Role of the Parent in Little League; Little*

League's Greatest Challenge by Arthur Esslinger, and *Happiness is Little League Baseball* by Thomas P. Johnson, M.D.

Magill, Richard. *Children and Youth in Sport: A Contemporary Anthology.* Edited by Richard A. Magill, Michael J. Ash, and Frank L. Smoll. Champagne, IL: Human Kinetics, Publishers, forthcoming Jan. 1978.

Michener, James A. *Sports in America.* New York: Random House, 1976.

Refreshing style and thorough research into sport. Michener poses some quite interesting questions for our society.

National Junior Tennis League, Inc., 500 East 62nd St., 21st Floor, New York, NY 10021.

Introduces "tennis to youth who would otherwise not be exposed, or have the opportunity, to play the game." An interesting note — the NJTL Board of Directors decided last year to discontinue the National Tournament (at Forest Hills) because of extreme pressure on the young players and problems in administering the program. It can be done!

Orlick, Terry and Botterill, Cal. *Every Kid Can Win.* Chicago: Nelson Hall, 1975.

Excellent material on cooperative games and good questions and answers about many of the current issues in sport for children and youth.

Parker, Thomas. Establishing communication, leadership, and motivation in youth sports. *The Weekend Coach,* June 1976.

Parker, who is an athlete and coach of youth, emphasizes the behavioral side of working with young children and the quality of leadership characteristics. Details in a very real way the problems and concerns of volunteer coaches.

Scanlon, Tara Kost. Children in competition: Examination of state anxiety and social comparison responses in the laboratory and in the field. Proceedings of the National Physical Education Association for Men and the National Association of Physical Education for College Women Joint Meeting, Orlando, Florida, 1977.

Ms. Scanlon, University of California, Los Angeles, has been conducting excellent research relative to youth soccer leagues in

California. She has presented her findings with implications for the practitioner at several meetings, AAHPER National Convention, Seattle, with Vern Seefeldt and Rainer Martens (tape available).

Seefeldt, Vern (Project Coordinator). *Joint Legislative Study on Youth Sports Programs*. Senators Carl D. Pursell and James E. O'Neill, Committee Co-Chairmen. State of Michigan, Nov. 18, 1976.

Details the status of youth sports programs in Michigan, raises many questions, and has a section entitled "Effects of Athletic Competition on Children and Youth" (Chapter 2). It is an excellent resource for any state legislature to use in forming resolutions.

Smoll, Frank and Smith, Ronald E. *Psychological Perspectives in Youth Sports*. Washington, DC: Hemisphere Publishing Co., forthcoming late 1977.

Tutko, Thomas and Burns, WIlliam. *Winning is Everything and Other American Myths*. New York: Macmillan, 1976.

YMCA. Youth Basketball Association (YBA) Program. New York, NY 10007, National Board of YMCAs, 1976.

YBA is a positive alternative to existing youth sports philosophy of "win at all costs," puts winning in proper perspective and emphasizes values and fair play. Materials are available, as are uniforms and the possible connection with NBA players. Coaches and player manuals are an excellent source for positive development of programs.